IRANIAN F-14 TOMCAT UNITS IN COMBAT

SERIES EDITOR: TONY HOLMES

OSPREY COMBAT AIRCRAFT • 49

RANIAN F-14 TOMCAT UNITS IN COMBAT

TOM COOPER AND FARZAD BISHOP

OSPREY
PUBLISHING

Cover caption
On 26 October 1980, two F-14A Tomcats of the Islamic Republic of Iran Air Force (IRIAF), flown by Maj Hazin and Capt Akhbari, engaged two Iraqi Air Force (IrAF) MiG-21MFs from Qalat Salih air base over Shahid Asaye, just north of Ahwaz. Hazin, now a lieutenant general, recalled what happened during the short air battle which ensued;

'We closed on the Iraqi MiG-21s undetected. Our aeroplanes were only armed with AIM-7s and AIM-9s, so we came in really close. I fired one AIM-9 at very close range, and when my missile hit the MiG, it blew up into a massive fireball almost immediately – I could not avoid the explosion. Parts of the disintegrating MiG-21 hit the left wing of my aircraft and were then ingested into the left engine. Fire warnings were blinking all around the cockpit. I lost power in that engine, and when I looked to the left I also realised that the AIM-7 and AIM-9 that had been mounted on the port wing shoulder pylon had been ripped away. The soot from the explosion of the MiG enveloped my jet as it passed through the fireball.

'Meanwhile, my wingman had engaged another MiG-21 and shot it down using two Sidewinders. He later reported that after seeing my F-14 exiting on the other side of the explosion, he was sure that it was badly burned and the crew dead.

'There were two other Iraqi MiGs nearby, but they dropped their bombs and turned back to Iraq, leaving their squadronmates to their fate. This was most fortunate for us, as I had great problems with the controls and the speed of my Tomcat. Capt Akhbari suggested we land at Ahwaz or Dezful, but I refused to do so. Both of these airfields could soon fall to the Iraqi Army, and I was not going to be responsible for handing an IRIAF F-14A to the enemy. So we decided to return to Khatami, where the jet could either be repaired or used as a spares source. If that was not possible, we could abandon the aircraft and let it crash into the Iranian desert. Despite the jet having suffered severe damage, and being difficult to control, we managed to get it safely back to Khatami. The F-14 was later repaired and returned to service' (*Cover artwork by Mark Postlethwaite*)

Dedication

Ten Iranian pilots and RIOs were killed while flying F-14A Tomcats in the defence of their country. This book is dedicated to their memory, and also to those who survived

First published in Great Britain in 2004 by Osprey Publishing,
Midland House, West Way, Botley, Oxford OX2 0PH, UK
443 Park Avenue South, New York, NY 10016, USA

CIP Data for this publication is available from the British Library

ISBN 978 1 84176 787 1

Edited by Tony Holmes and Bruce Hales-Dutton
Page design by Tony Truscott
Cover Artwork by Mark Postlethwaite
Aircraft Profiles by Jim Laurier
Scale Drawings by Mark Styling
Index by David Worthington
Originated by PPS Grasmere Ltd., Leeds, UK
Printed and bound in China through Bookbuilders
08 09 10 11 12   12 11 10 9 8 7 6 5 4

FOR A CATALOGUE OF ALL BOOKS PUBLISHED BY OSPREY PLEASE CONTACT:
NORTH AMERICA
Osprey Direct, C/o Random House Distribution Centre, 400 Hahn Road, Westminster. MD 21157
E-mail:info@ospreydirect.com

ALL OTHER REGIONS
Osprey Direct, The Book Service Ltd, Distribution Centre, Colchester Road, Frating Green, Colchester, Essex, CO7 7DW
E-mail: customerservice@ospreypublishing.com

ACKNOWLEDGMENTS
The authors wish to express their gratitude to all those serving and retired officers of both the Imperial Iranian Air Force (IIAF) and the Islamic Republic of Iran Air Force (IRIAF), too many of whom are sadly no longer with us. A special thank you to the 'Last of the First', as well as all those who gave interviews or provided help and information. We sincerely hope that this work will end the injustices done to the Iranian Tomcat crews in respect to the incorrect reporting of their feats in combat during the Iran–Iraq conflict. Special thanks also to 'Tom N', whose research has proven indispensable in the compilation of this volume. Finally, thank you to our long-suffering families who have supported us throughout our many years of research into the IIAF and the IRIAF.

www.ospreypublishing.com

CONTENTS

INTRODUCTION

I n the summer of 1972, a letter from Mohammad-Reza Pahlavi, *Shahanshah* (King of Kings) and ruler of Iran, arrived at the Pentagon in Washington, DC. It announced his intention of visiting the USA to be briefed on the interceptor aircraft about to enter service with both the US Navy and Air Force. He also planned to watch flying demonstrations of these new fighter types, with the intention of acquiring examples for his favourite branch of the Iranian armed forces, the Imperial Iranian Air Force (IIAF). The main object of his interest was Grumman's F-14A Tomcat.

This visit marked the beginning of a highly controversial arms sale that was to lead to the deployment by Iran of the most modern combat aircraft supplied to any US ally. This was the first time that the Americans had agreed to sell such advanced military hardware to a foreign customer. It also represented a bold move by Iran, for it was about to integrate a complex weapons system into a military organisation still gaining experience with high-technology systems, and the infrastructure necessary to ensure their successful operation.

The foreign sale of the aircraft also meant that the whole F-14 project was rescued by Iran when it agreed to lend the Grumman Corporation the money it needed to continue Tomcat production. But the F-14's service in Iran was to become characterised by an implausible series of controversies, 'educated guesstimates' that turned out to be completely wrong and not a few wild rumours based mainly on Western ignorance of the IRIAF's true capabilities. The full background as to why this occurred is not yet clear, but it is obvious that in assessing the F-14A/AWG-9/AIM-54 system in combat, the performance of the Tomcat in Iranian service and making the comparison with contemporary interceptors and fighter-bombers, most observers have failed to offer an objective insight. Indeed, reports published to date border on fiction rather than fact.

Similar behaviour was experienced by former Iranian F-14 pilots after they fled to the West in the wake of the 1979 revolution. Their combat accounts were generally mistrusted regardless of the available evidence. Even if they received congratulations – off the record – for their achievements, most official reaction betrayed the West's inability to believe the extent of the F-14's use by the IRIAF. Typical of this was the US Navy's stubborn refusal to accept that the Iranians could deploy the F-14, and its associated AWG-9 radar and AIM-54A Phoenix missiles, effectively in combat. In fact, none of the active or former US Navy pilots or Radar Intercept Officers interviewed by the authors believed Iran still operated the Tomcat, or that its personnel were able to master its associated systems. The reaction of one when shown a photograph of an F-14 in Iranian colours – taken only weeks before – is characteristic: 'Yeah . . . and it's on the ground!'

Up until the publication of this volume, there has been no serious effort made by aviation historians to use authentic sources to research the history of the Iranian F-14 programme. Neither the many former Iranian pilots living in exile or those who remain in Iran had ever been asked about their experiences. The few media reports published in Iran were completely ignored outside the country, and Iranian F-14 pilots, active or retired, remained bemused by what was reported in the Western press.

The results of this mis-reporting are obvious. The true role of the F-14 in Iranian service – particularly during the war with Iraq – remains unknown. Furthermore, the lack of information about the combat performance of the AWG-9/AIM-54 weapons system resulted in the US Navy making a number of controversial decisions in respect to its employment of the F-14 in fleet service.

This book offers the first in-depth insight into the Tomcat's service with the IRIAF. It is primarily based on a series of exhaustive interviews with retired and active Iranian F-14 pilots and RIOs, and with several ex-Iraqi Air Force officers. In addition, the authors have also drawn from official US, Iranian, Saudi and Soviet documents released to them. The resulting story shows that Iranian aircrews were not only brave and capable in combat, but that they were backed up by groundcrews who also deserve the highest respect for their technical fortitude.

Tom Cooper & Farzad Bishop
Austria, June 2004

THE REQUIREMENT

I ran's inability to prevent overflights by Soviet MiG-25Rs is said by many Western observers to have been one of the main reasons why the country acquired the Grumman F-14. The truth is slightly different, however. Since the late 1950s, the Imperial Iranian Air Force (IIAF), in cooperation with the USAF, had been flying highly secret reconnaissance flights over the USSR. Initially, lighter aircraft (even transports) were used, and several were shot down by Soviet fighters. After the first F-4s arrived, the IIAF also received some RF-4Es (see *Combat Aircraft 37* for details), and operations were intensified.

The Soviets were, understandably, concerned about Iran's massive re-armament, and started their own reconnaissance missions over the country. IIAF interceptors – especially F-4Ds – repeatedly tried to catch the MiG-25Rs, but this proved a very difficult task as the routes flown by the overflying 'Foxbats' were carefully chosen.

The Shah was not interested in a direct confrontation with the USSR, so as the mutual airspace violations intensified, he offered to stop IIAF – and American – overflights if the Soviets would do the same. This offer was repeated, and turned down, several times. The IIAF was therefore ordered to fly two or more missions over the USSR for every 'Foxbat' flight, initiating a 'tit for tat' campaign. But a more powerful weapon system than Sparrow-armed F-4s was needed to prevent Soviet incursions.

Meanwhile, in line with plans for massive Iranian military development during the 1970s, as well as future cooperation with the USA, the IIAF was seeking a new interceptor that was able to meet foreseeable threats over the next 20 years. It would have to cover huge areas of Iranian airspace using powerful sensors and weaponry, and have a corresponding endurance and combat ability.

COMPETITION AND SELECTION

As early as 1968, the IIAF had expressed an interest in the General Dynamics F-111, but the Pentagon was not keen, preferring instead to sell Iran 32 McDonnell Douglas F-4D Phantom IIs. The Pentagon subsequently had to issue a requirement for a new naval interceptor as a result of the unsuitability of the projected F-111B for carrier operations in light of Vietnam combat experience.

In response, the Grumman Corporation designed the F-14 Tomcat as a specialised 'MiG killer'. It was a large, fast and powerful interceptor, with wings that could be automatically swept between 14 and 68 degrees for increased endurance, flexibility and manoeuvrability in air combat against small and nimble MiGs. It was also designed to carry the huge

AN/AWG-9 pulse-Doppler radar and up to six long-range Hughes AIM-54 Phoenix air-to-air missiles, which were required by the US Navy to intercept the formations of Soviet bombers considered to pose the greatest threat to its fleet of aircraft carriers.

F-14A BuNo 160299 was the very first Tomcat built for Iran, and it is seen here soon after being rolled out of the Grumman plant at Calverton, New York, in 1975 (*Grumman via authors*)

The Tomcat's AWG-9 radar and AIM-54 missile had already been in development for some years, and now they had become highly effective. So much so that the radar could not only detect airborne targets over vast distances, but also simultaneously track up to 24 targets and guide six AIM-54s against them. It also permitted the interception of low flying cruise missiles, as well as high and fast-flying targets like the MiG-25.

All these abilities were combined in a single airframe to produce the world's first 'superfighter' – an interceptor able to confront most threats. It was also the most costly and complex fighter built to date. It was not long, therefore, before controversy arose in the US resulting from development problems, cost overruns (caused by rampant inflation) and a debate centring on whether such an expensive aircraft was needed at all. As a result, both Grumman and the US Navy were seeking an additional customer to share the cost of further development and production.

By October 1971, Grumman had established the first contacts with the Iranian government, and the following March Gen Hassan Toufanian was allowed to see secret information pertaining to the F-14. Toufanian was a military advisor to the Shah, as well as Deputy Minister of War and Director of the Arms Industries and Military Procurement Organisation. Soon, the Shah himself was showing an interest in the aircraft.

In agreement with the IIAF leadership – which had already concluded that the F-14 was the interceptor it was seeking – a letter was sent to the Pentagon to start the acquisition process, although the Iranians still offered McDonnell Douglas the chance to demonstrate its F-15A Eagle.

Early F-14 pilot Capt Rassi (the names of all F-14 pilots and RIOs interviewed for this book, active or retired, have been changed for security reasons) explained why the Iranians were so interested in the Tomcat:

'There were several factors which influenced the selection of the F-14. Iran's northern border with the USSR, and those to the west and southwest with Iraq, are guarded by high mountains. Our Air Defence Command was building radar outposts on many peaks for better radar coverage, but we could never improve the situation with ground-based radar alone. There were too many "blind spots" in this coverage, and the big white domes of our radar stations were also excellent targets, visible from up to 50 miles away. Intelligence information obtained at the time verified that the Soviets would indeed strike them first.

'In the south, along the Persian Gulf coast, we had only US-supplied radars, which did not work properly in hot and humid conditions – that is, for ten months of the year – and otherwise also had poor performance, despite several upgrades. All the radars supplied to the IIAF as part of Military Assistance Program projects were far from being top-of-the-line. The Americans gave us what they wanted to give, not what we needed.

'For two years – 1973–74 – a group of Iranian radar instructors, including Col Iradj Ghaffari (the first Iranian tactical radar instructor), studied coverage problems associated with "Radar Sites Reinforcement", but could not find a solution. Eventually, it was decided that a "flying radar" would eliminate the terrain masking problems. That flying radar would also have to be able to defend itself. It is beyond doubt that during the war with Iraq, the F-14 proved that it was exactly what we needed.

'Before these studies were conducted within IIAF circles – at the time we were still flying F-5A/B Freedom Fighters and F-4D Phantom IIs – we started looking for a top-of-the-line fighter interceptor. The result of these studies, directed by Gen Mehdi Rouhani, was a requirement for F-14s and AEW aircraft. US briefings on F-14s and F-15s undoubtedly helped us to formulate our requirement. We created the plan to purchase eight AEW aircraft – initially four, followed by four more – and the F-14s. Eventually, four orders were issued – the first for 30 Tomcats and the second for 50. There was one for Boeing E-3 Sentry AWACS, followed by one for two communication satellites, which would enable all these aircraft to communicate securely with each other.'

Unaware that the Iranians had already identified the F-14 as the right aircraft for their unique operational requirements, the US Navy and Grumman started an intensive campaign to 'sell the Shah', which included sending the F-14 Program Coordinator of the Chief of Naval Operations, Capt Mitchell, to Tehran twice to brief the Shah and IIAF commanders on the Tomcat's capabilities. This culminated in a spectacular fly-off in July 1973 at Andrews AFB, Maryland, for the Shah and a group of high-ranking Iranian officers.

While many US officials and Navy officers still believe that this stunning show put on by Grumman test pilots influenced the Shah's final decision to order the F-14, Iranian officers interviewed by the authors strongly disagree. One of the first to fly the Tomcat was Maj Ali. He had experience of the F-4, as well as having exchange tours with the USAF, Israeli Defence Force /Air Force (IDF/AF), Luftwaffe, US Navy, RAF and Pakistani Air Force to his credit. He was later to score more than five aerial victories against Iraq, and he offered a further insight into the background to the Iranian order:

'Both the IIAF and the Shah had studied the F-14A and the F-15A since their inception. In 1972, very early on in our studies, we learned that the F-15A with the AIM-7F missile was to be a deadly fighter-weapon mix, but not as deadly as the AIM-54-armed F-14A. It was clear to us that the F-14/AWG-9 pulse-Doppler radar/AIM-54 combination would be unequalled in the world – which it remains today. The AWG-9 enabled us to engage at ranges that F-15 pilots could only dream of. We could even use AIM-7s and AIM-9s at longer ranges than the Eagle. Yet this complex radar and weapons system was simple to operate. It took much practice and hard work to operate the weapon systems in

With afterburners blazing and the provisional serial 3-863 applied to its fin, BuNo 160299 takes off on its inaugural flight on 5 December 1975. Interestingly, this serial, applied mainly for publicity purposes, was to cause many observers to believe that the first 30 Tomcats supplied to Iran were numbered 3-863 to 3-912, which was not the case (*authors' collection*)

the F-15A, and the USAF had still to clear these initial problems with the man-machine interface – especially the Head-Up Display – and this did not happen before the mid 1970s.

'Of course, we were most impressed by both fighters. They had great visibility from their roomy cockpits, were built specifically for fighter pilots and had excellent state-of-the art avionics, powerful engines and excellent manoeuvrability. Both boasted precise target tracking during air combat and had no real angle of attack (AOA) limits, except in training.

'The F-15A was pleasant to fly due to its flight control augmentation system, which was a major improvement at the time. However, we also concluded early on that the F-15A would not be as manoeuvrable or as flexible as the F-14A. The Tomcat has very straightforward flight characteristics, but is highly agile. The pilot enjoys manoeuvrability to an extent previously only dreamed of. The jet's variable sweep wings and aerofoil qualities give it a great advantage when manoeuvring. At low level and at low or supersonic speeds, with pilots of equal skill, the F-14A always wins against the F-15A. I know this as a matter of fact – I was later to fly F-15As with the USAF in mock-dogfights against US Navy F-14As.

'The capability of the F-14A to snap around during the dogfight was unequalled at the time. Even today, I'm sure that anything but the F/A-18 or F-22 would be hard pressed to beat it. After only 100 hours of training I learned to pitch the nose of my F-14 up at 75 degrees AOA in just over a second, turn around and acquire my opponent either with the AIM-9 or the gun.

'The F-14's only weak point was its TF30 engines, which were unreliable. We had to learn to fly them – not the airframe. The engines were always a problem on the F-14. Nevertheless, under certain flight conditions they develop just over 20,000 lbs of thrust each. That's enough for the

The 'Asia Minor' camouflage pattern applied uniformly to all Iranian F-14As was laid down in order TO 1-1-4, which required uppersurfaces to be painted in tan FS20400, dark green FS34079 and brown FS30140, while all lower and undersurfaces were painted in grey FS36622. Note that the leading edges of the wings, horizontal stabilators and vertical stabilisers have been left unpainted (*Grumman via authors*)

Preliminary negotiations between the IIAF and Pratt & Whitney to re-equip Iranian Tomcats with more powerful and reliable F100 or F401 engines came to nothing, so the aircraft has had to soldier on with the unreliable and oversensitive TF30 – shown here – to this day. So far, no less than nine aircraft have been lost in engine-related accidents, including 3-6013 and 3-6048 as early as 1977 (*authors' collection*)

F-14A to stand on its tail and hold an indicated airspeed below 85 mph and 40 degrees AOA. This is possible due to the large "stabilators" – a combination of elevators and horizontal stabilisers. Dual rudders for directional control also provide roll control at medium and high AOA.'

IIAF studies were indicating these advantages, and the Shah – himself an experienced pilot – got them confirmed during briefings by US Navy officers. Very soon there was little doubt about which aircraft would be acquired. Rassi concluded:

'We couldn't care less about what some in the US called "selling" the F-14s to Iran. It's totally naive to believe that a show organised for the Shah would make any reasonable and responsible person decide to spend billions of dollars, train thousands of personnel, spend additional millions to build support facilities and thereby influence the future of the whole air force for the following 30 years on the basis of "the F-14 display was better than the F-15"! No way. We knew better than to be influenced by the stunts of American pilots.

'We were searching not only for a fighter superior in manoeuvrability and weaponry, but also for a highly flexible area defence interceptor. We wanted a complete system, including superior sensors, effective long-range weapons and man-machine interface that would need little or no outside support. We simply couldn't ignore the F-14. Its performance during the war with Iraq confirmed our decision beyond any doubt.'

DELIVERY AND TRAINING

The $300m Project *Persian King* contract, covering delivery of the first 30 F-14A-GR Tomcats, was signed on 7 January 1974. It included a large quantity of spare parts, replacement engines and a complete armament package, including 424 AIM-54As. A few months later, in June 1974, the IIAF ordered another 50 F-14As and a further 290 Phoenix missiles. The bill for *Persian King* finally totalled $2bn, and it was considered at the time to be the highest value single foreign military sale in US history.

Soon, the Iranian order was to save the whole Tomcat project, as well as Grumman itself. Not only did it come at a time when the F-14 was getting a lot of bad press due to cost overruns and schedule slippage, but the Iranians also made it clear that they thought that the F-14 was a far better air superiority system than the F-15.

In August 1974, while Grumman was producing the first significant batches of Tomcats for the US Navy and Iran, the US Congress blocked the financing of the whole programme. Grumman was on the verge of bankruptcy, but the Shah ordered the Iranian bank Melli to lend the company the money needed to fulfil the IIAF order. Other investors were also encouraged to make loans. Had it not been for this timely injection of Iranian cash, the whole F-14 programme could have easily been terminated, thus robbing the US Navy of its principal fleet fighter.

Once built, Iranian Tomcats received a different camouflage scheme to their Navy brethren, but internally there was little to choose between them. It is often said that the ECM and ECCM systems of Iranian F-14s were downgraded, but as Maj Ali explains, this was not the case:

'There are so many publications in the West claiming that the AWG-9s and AIM-54s supplied to Iran were of a poor standard, lacking the ECM suite built into the examples delivered to the US Navy. Such reports are worthless, as the AWG-9 radars and AIM-54s sold to Iran had exactly the same specifications and capabilities as their US Navy counterparts. They were, and still are, of the highest standard. There's only one minor difference – the speed at which the AWG-9 and the AIM-54 radars changed their working frequency, or jumped wavelengths to counter jamming, was slightly slower on our systems.

'This was a politically motivated change introduced to quieten those opposed to the sale of F-14s, and similar highly sensitive systems, to Iran. The modification meant that the Navy could legitimately tell Congress that the systems supplied to Iran were less capable than those used by the US military. In reality, the processors mounted in our jets were barely 1/100th of second slower than those used in Navy F-14s.

'Obviously, these are things not talked about openly, but to me it's still a mystery that anybody could seriously believe that we would be foolish enough to accept grossly downgraded aircraft and weapons that could not be used to their fullest capability – and pay billions of dollars for them!'

Indeed, Iranian Tomcats were even equipped with the 'top secret' APX-81-M1E (designated APX-82-A in US Navy service) IFF (identification friend/foe) interrogator. This 'Combat Tree' equipment was not only capable of detecting enemy aircraft without the help of radar by interrogating their IFF, but could also supply data such as true airspeed and accurate ranging. The only difference between the APX-81-M1E and similar systems fitted into the Navy F-14s was that the Iranian equipment could only detect and interrogate IFF transponders of Soviet origin.

Unlike Navy F-14s, however, Iranian jets were never equipped with the AN/ALR-23 IRST (infra-red scanner/tracker) system mounted under the aircraft's radome, even if the first Tomcat built for Iran (BuNo 160299) was frequently shown carrying one. Maj Ali recalls:

'The Pentagon seriously tried to sell the ALR-23 to Iran, but the IIAF knew that the system had a very limited range, provided data of limited quality and frequently misidentified sources of IR emissions.'

Instead, the IIAF, having seen the excellent results achieved with the ASX-1 TISEO electro-optical sensor fitted to its late-build F-4Es, opted to wait for the more capable Northrop AN/AXX-1 Television Camera Set (TCS) to enter service. However, by the time this system was declared operational in the early 1980s the revolution had seen the Shah deposed and the US turn its back on its former ally.

Iranian F-14s also lacked the AN/ARA-62 instrument landing system optimised for carrier recoveries, as well as the KIT-1A, KIR-1A and KY-28 coding/decoding equipment. Finally, the AIM-54As delivered to Iran had their ECCM suites downgraded to make them less effective in combat against US-built aircraft and their ECM systems.

F-14As for Iran are assembled alongside US Navy Tomcats and A-6E Intruders. Here, one of the future 'Ali-Cats' is seen in the final stages of completion at Calverton. Other than the camouflage colours, the only external difference between an Iranian and US Navy Tomcat was the absence of the refuelling probe bay doors on the IIAF jet. These were deleted before delivery in accordance with Iranian wishes when the IIAF learned that the doors could come away and cause damage to the fuselage during in-flight refuelling (*Grumman via authors*)

A close-up view of the 20 mm General Electric M61A1 Vulcan cannon, the weapon's six rotating barrels, its gun-drive motor and the ammunition drum, which held a maximum of 675 rounds. The cannon has a maximum rate of fire of 6000 rounds per minute at a muzzle velocity of 3400 ft per minute. Also visible is the stencilling around the cockpit. All warning stencils applied to Iranian Tomcats are written in English, and are therefore identical to those worn on US Navy F-14s (*authors' collection*)

These pilots and RIOs from the 81st TFW were some of the first aircrew to convert onto the F-14A. None can be identified by name due to security concerns (*IIAF Association*)

On the credit side, all Iranian Tomcats got the USAF-style seat harness locks, diluter-demand oxygen system and oxygen masks – IIAF pilots considered the latter to be more comfortable than its US Navy equivalent. Finally, Iranian F-14s were powered by TF30-PW-414 engines, which were less stall-prone than the earlier TF30-PW-412s, although they could still be temperamental, and trailed smoke at maximum dry thrust

Prior to the F-14s' arrival in Iran, a large new air base was built in the desert near Esfahan. Known as Tactical Fighter Base 8 (TFB 8), it was named Khatami in memory of legendary IIAF Commander-in-Chief Gen Khatami, who had been killed in a gliding accident on 12 September 1975. The base became the main hub for Tomcat operations in Iran, with the first two units equipped with the type (the 81st and 82nd Tactical Fighter Squadrons) being stationed there. The 71st and 72nd TFSs were formed at TFB 7, near Shiraz. Maj Rassi recalled:

'Contrary to what is usually published, the training of Iranian F-14 crews also proceeded at a rapid pace. Mr Clark of Grumman liaised between the IIAF, the US Navy and the company. He organised the first team of 14 Grumman and US Navy pilots and technicians that were sent to Iran to help prepare the IIAF for the introduction of Tomcats into service. They inspected future bases, met local commanders and some of their future students and then put together a training syllabus. In the IIAF, the F-14 project liaison officer was Col S Glaze, whose boss was Gen Gohary, who in turn reported to Gen Toufanian.'

In May 1974 the first group of four highly experienced Iranian F-4 pilots arrived at NAS Miramar, California, to begin their training on the F-14 with the Navy's West Coast F-14 training unit, VF-124 'Gunfighters'. They were Gen Abdol Hossein Minousepehr (who became CO of the IIAF's 8th Tactical Fighter Wing, and also head of the F-14 programme), Majs Mojtaba Zangeneh and Mohamad Farvahar and Capt Karan Heidarzadeh. They were to become the first Iranian F-14 instructors. In addition, Zangeneh was the IIAF officer given the job of testing the AIM-54 Phoenix missile in the US.

One month later the second group of 80 officers arrived at NAS Oceana, Virginia, for training with the Navy's East Coast F-14 training unit, VF-101 'Grim Reapers'.

This group consisted of 11 more pilots, all of captain rank – Hassan Afghantoloee, Jamshid Afshar, Abbas Amiraslani, Reza Attaee, Bahram Ghaneii, Abolfazl Hoosh-yar, Jalil Moslemi, Mohamad Pirasteh, Shahram Rostami, Javad Shokraii and Hossein Taghdis. They were accompanied by a small group of technicians.

Other Iranian groundcrewmen went to Pratt & Whitney to learn how to maintain and support the TF30 engine, while 26 engineers were sent to the Weapons Division of Hughes Aircraft Corporation to begin training and classroom studies on the AWG-9 radar and associated systems, as well as the AIM-54A Phoenix missile.

The first four US F-14 instructors arrived in Iran in November 1975. After inspecting installations and preparing a training plan, they returned home for a refresher course before delivering the aircraft. From late April 1976 through to February 1979, 27 American instructor pilots were permanently stationed at Khatami, together with other Grumman employees. They were led by Grumman's L A Senead and C Zangas (both former US Navy officers), who were directly answerable to USAF Gen R Huyer, head of the US Military Mission to Iran.

These three photographs show the control tower, elaborate ground support infrastructure and giant hardened aircraft shelters (each able to house up to two F-14s) constructed at Khatami air base specially for the Tomcat. Built in the desert outside Esfahan, in central Iran, the base's sole purpose was to be the main operational hub for Iranian F-14 operations (*IIAF Association via authors*)

In March 1976, as Col Marandi became CO of Khatami, a second large group of Iranian pilots – led by IIAF Col M Rostami and US Navy Lt Cdr Dave Chew – arrived at NAS Miramar to re-qualify on the F-14A. This group not only completed the training in record time, it also participated in several joint exercises with the US Navy, USAF, USMC and ANG.

By December 1976 most of the training of groundcrews had been completed. In just two years, between 110 and 120 crews had been fully qualified, and a further 100 were in training, some 20 of whom were just short of final qualification. Nevertheless, during the early stages of the F-14's career in Iran, considerable problems were experienced with the maintenance of this very complex fighter. Grumman established training teams to teach Iranian students troubleshooting methods and procedures that did not tie up, or damage, the servicing equipment. These teams operated exclusively in the US, however. Maj Ali explained:

'The Americans would not teach our technical staff anything sensitive about the Tomcats avionics, and they wouldn't let us do anything alone.

The Pentagon would not permit any of the "sensitive" systems to be repaired or maintained in Iran, nor would it train our technicians to maintain and repair them. All such parts had to be packed and sent to the US for maintenance and repair at a huge cost to us. It also meant that at any one time, a large number of IIAF F-14s were grounded in the years leading up to the revolution.'

The third IIAF unit to receive F-14s was the 73rd TFS, which became operational at TFB 7 Shiraz in 1977. The unit's F-14As 3-6063 (foreground) and 3-6052 both display the TFB number on their fin – a small black seven inside a black circle. Iranian Tomcats have never been as brightly marked as those flown by the US Navy. Indeed, the TFB numbers and serials were the only addition until after the revolution (*US DoD via authors*)

In an effort to improve these maintenance problems, a complex and expensive computer-supported logistical infrastructure called Peace Log was developed to facilitate the organisation, procurement and shipment of spare parts and weapons from different companies in the US to Iran. The main concern of the Americans, however, was to keep the Tomcat, and its many sensitive systems, secret at any price – regardless of the cost to the IIAF.

The other major technical problem experienced during Project *Persian King* centred on the Tomcat's engines. The TF30 was originally expected to be an interim and cheap powerplant solution until a more suitable replacement – expected in service by the mid-1970s – could be found. The new engine project was subsequently cancelled due to a lack of funds, by which time the TF30-PW-412 had already started to cause major problems even after it had been upgraded to -414 specification in an effort to make it less stall-prone. Engine stalls caused the loss of two F-14As, and the death of an Iranian pilot, in early air combat training.

The IIAF knew about the weakness of the Tomcat's engines, and it was quick to open private negotiations with Pratt & Whitney for the replacement of the TF30s. This was particularly important, as in 1976 Iran had issued a letter of intent to purchase 70 additional F-14s.

Iranian F-14As H6 (foreground, BuNo 160304 and IIAF serial 3-6006) and H4 (rear, BuNo 160302 and IIAF serial 3-6004) head a line up of newly built Tomcats on the tarmac at Calverton shortly before their delivery flight to Iran. More details of the camouflage pattern on the jets' uppersurfaces are revealed from this elevated angle (*Grumman via authors*)

Despite these engine maladies, the F-14 was still an impressive machine, the likes of which had never previously been flown by IIAF pilots such as Capt Javad:

'As a former F-4 pilot, I found the F-14A light years ahead right from the start of my training. I had no problems in leaving my Phantom II squadron for a new Tomcat unit. I loved the Phantom II, but learned to love the F-14A even more. Every pilot falls in love with an aircraft or two during his career, but there will always be one favourite, and mine was without a doubt the desert-camouflaged F-14 marked with the flag of my beloved country, and carrying the markings of the IIAF.

'When I touched it for the first time I was overcome with pride, and I felt honoured to be part of the programme. At that very moment the Shah and the IIAF commander arrived to inspect the very same Tomcat I was climbing into. His Majesty saw me and three other pilots admiring our new aircraft. He approached us and, after we saluted, he asked me, "Captain, what do you think of our newest fighter?"

'I replied that I couldn't think of a better fighter in the world to defend Iran than the F-14 Tomcat. The Shah smiled and then went on to tell me, "Captain, there is no better fighter in the world, and that is exactly why we have them in our air force. However, Captain, I must give you an order that will challenge you and place a great burden on your shoulders, and the shoulders of your colleagues – master the Tomcat and its weapons systems without delay. The F-14, and its advanced systems, will never be better than the pilots we trust to fly them in defence of our nation. So, you Captain, must always strive to be the best."

'And so I did, as well as the whole squadron. Our training on the F-14 went well – fast, and without problems. I found the cockpit well laid out, and the view from the front and back seats vastly improved over the F-4. The cockpit was comfortable, and somehow familiar – probably because both the Phantom II and the Tomcat were built for the US Navy. The 20 mm cannon and AIM-7 and AIM-9 systems were all known to me. I only had to train intensively on the AIM-54 system.'

While some US instructors have frequently said that the F-14 project suffered from a lack of suitable IIAF personnel, and thus proceeded at a very slow pace, the IIAF's hand-picked crews actually got the type into operational service in a very reasonable time, as Maj Rassi recalled:

'We soon completed our basic training and went on to learn how to fly and fight in combat. During dissimilar air combat training against our F-5E Tiger IIs and F-4 Phantom IIs we were never defeated. Even when taking on four F-4Es with slatted wings, a lone Tomcat won within a matter of a few minutes. There was nothing in our air force – or, later, in the Iraqi Air Force – that I couldn't out-turn in my Tomcat.'

Maj Ali added:

'The Shah and our commanders were increasingly worried about the overflights of Soviet MiG-25s. Each time our F-4s failed to intercept one

A close up of H29 (BuNo 160327 and later 3-6029) with the provisional US markings applied in preparation for its delivery flight to Iran. Note that the refuelling bay doors have not yet been removed, and also the way the brown camouflage colour has been applied around the right intake (*Grumman, via authors*)

of the Russian intruders we tried something new. We came closer and closer, and in 1975 a MiG-25R was finally damaged by a Sparrow, but the jet made it back over the border before crashing. This was a dangerous game, however, for the Soviets downed one of our RF-4s soon afterwards.

'The situation became very tense, and in 1976 the IIAF purchased six AQM-37 target drones from an Italian company and put us, and our brand new F-14s, to the test. Of the five drones launched by Phantom IIs, which simulated MiG-25s flying at speed and altitude, four were shot down by AIM-54s. One Phoenix missed due to a systems failure. A few weeks later one of our F-14s intercepted a Soviet MiG-25R and locked it up with the AWG-9 radar while the Russian was at 65,000 ft flying at Mach 2+. The Soviets immediately stopped their overflights, and we did the same by mutual agreement. But that was neither the end of our training, nor the end of our trial Phoenix firings.'

As part of their US training, pilots visited Hughes, where AIM-54As missiles designated for the IIAF were built. One of them recalled:

'During the visit in 1976 I was able to see the assembly line for Iranian AIM-54As as well as that for the US Navy. Our missiles were being hand-built at a very, very slow pace, yet the Navy line was impressive, with at least 40 AIM-54s being in different stages of completion.'

Some 714 AIM-54As were ordered by the IIAF but only 284 were delivered, including ten training rounds. Another 40 were ready for shipment when the revolution brought *Persian King* to an abrupt end. Maj Nuzran, another highly-experienced and combat-proven pilot who was later to down four MiG-23s during a single engagement, explained;

'The AIM-54 was a truly deadly system, and there is nothing that can match its performances in service today. Much was said later about different air-to-air missiles, their speed and manoeuvrability. But during testing in Iran in 1978 we tracked an AIM-54A at Mach 4.4 and 24,000 m (79,000 ft) before it scored a direct hit on a target drone. This large and hefty missile had no snap-up or snap-down limits, and could manoeuvre at up to 17g. We also tested it against targets at ranges down to only 7.5 km (four miles), and during another test in early 1979, we tracked an AIM-54A flying out to 212 km (114.5 miles), which may be an unofficial world record. The only problem with this weapon was maintenance – the Phoenix is a very complex system.'

Much has been written about the F-14's ability to fire six AIM-54s simultaneously. From a pilot's standpoint, Maj Ali had little doubt about the jet's capabilities when carrying such a load:

'We seldom loaded our Tomcats with six AIM-54s. I saw F-14s armed that way only twice in my career, and that was before the war with Iraq. In May 1978, I flew a Tomcat armed with six AIM-54s, and I was surprised to see just how much of an impact these large and heavy missiles had on the speed, range and manoeuvrability of the jet as a result of their weight and drag.

BuNo 160314 (later 3-6016) was photographed at Calverton at the same time as BuNo 160327 seen opposite (*Grumman, via authors*)

An F-14 loaded with six AIM-54s could not dogfight, and its landing speed was much higher – closer to 290 kmh (normally 230 kmh or 144 mph), which posed a danger to both the aircraft and its crew.'

Although capable of long-range shoot downs thanks to the AIM-54, the Tomcat was also a superb dogfighter. Here, Capt Rassi recalls what his Navy instructors told him about close-quarters fighting with the F-14:

'When the Americans trained us to dogfight with the F-4, they told us, "Always keep your enemy in sight, and if attacked, it's not always best to evade your opponent by running away. Meet your opponent head on, as it is easier to defeat an incoming missile approaching from head-on than from behind". When they trained us on F-14s, however, they said, "Keep your opponent in sight and take the offensive, as it's easy to do that with the F-14. Stay on your opponent's tail where you can shoot at him, and he can't fire back." Quite a difference. And we learned this lesson well.

'During the war, I encountered Iraqi MiG-21s and Mirages with their new Magic air-to-air missiles, but I could either attack and shoot them down before they saw me, or hold a tight turn at just above the stall and force anybody to overshoot. Then – no matter who the opponent – I could bring the nose around, go to full afterburner to regain energy and bring my jet into a firing position. The Sidewinder and the Vulcan gun proved perfect weapons during mock dogfights, and during the war too.'

Maj Ali concluded:

'We trained with Navy pilots who had "shot down" USAF and Israeli F-15s and F-16s almost at will in exercises over the years. They trained us well. Later, we also out-flew the much newer MiG-29s, which the IRIAF purchased in 1990 – that is why the IRIAF bought only a few of them.'

In addition to AIM-54As, Iranian F-14s were armed with AIM-9P Sidewinders, of which 800+ were purchased. Although Iran was cleared to receive AIM-7Fs, none were delivered as the IIAF intended to use AIM-54As for both medium and long-range air combat. Nevertheless, the Iranians acquired as many AIM-7E-2s and AIM-7E-4s as possible, the latter being a special version of the Sparrow compatible with the AWG-9.

To support the F-14s as well as the F-4s, the IIAF also purchased 14 Boeing KC 707-3J9C tankers between 1974 and 1978. Six were equipped with booms only for in-flight refuelling (IFR), but from 1976 six others had Beech Model 1800 drogue-equipped wingtip refuelling stores fitted. These were purchased specifically to support the Tomcats

BuNo 100327, photographed on its delivery flight, shows further details of the camouflage pattern applied to both the right side of the rear fuselage and the left fin. As previously mentioned, this Tomcat became 3-6029 in Iranian service, and its final fate remains unknown. Carrying temporary US markings, the Tomcats were flown from Bethpage to Iran via Rota, in Spain, and Turkey. They were supported en route by USAF Boeing KC-135 tankers. The US insignia was usually replaced by Iranian markings within minutes of the jet's arrival in Iran. Seen over the mountains on the Turkish–Iranian border, this particular aircraft's delivery flight originated not from Bethpage but from Grumman's test airfield at Calverton. Despite rumours to the contrary, Project *Persian King* was executed at considerable speed both in America and Iran. Indeed, the first aircraft were delivered barely two years after the initial order, despite their complexity and Grumman's financial problems (*authors' collection*)

which used the US Navy's IFR system. During the same project, the first six KC 707s supplied were also retrofitted to carry these pods. Additionally, during Project *Roving Eye* two KC 707s were equipped as ELINT/SIGINT reconnaissance platforms, and these monitored enemy electronic emissions, air defence system activity and radio communications. But, as Maj Nuzran recalled:

'In the 1970s, many of the IIAF's KC 707s were flown by American pilots under contract. This was later to cause problems, as during the war with Iraq the IRIAF was only capable of keeping six KC 707s operational. Two, configured as transports, stood on almost permanent alert, ready to fly wherever needed in the world to pick up spares purchased clandestinely for the IRIAF.'

H-56 (BuNo 160354) breaks into the pattern overhead TFB 1 on finals. Note the vortices developing along the leading edge of the wings as the aircraft turns tightly in the moist air. Also of interest is the camouflage pattern on the uppersurfaces of the aircraft, the details of which are not often shown (*authors' collection*)

THE REVOLUTION

Many published reports indicate that during and after the Islamic Revolution 'all the best' Iranian F-14 pilots had either left the country or been arrested and jailed. Some were even said to have been executed by the new clerical regime. Yet despite the unrest, the revolution and threats to their own safety and that of their families, only 27 fully qualified F-14 pilots left Iran. This number included all but two of the original cadre and 15 pilots still in training. Some had fled the country with their families even before the Shah and the Americans had left, while others remained in Iran, waiting to see what would happen.

The F-14 pilots were all hand-picked for the job, being exceptional fliers with great experience. They also represented the cream of Iranian society, and to the last man they were patriots. Consequently, most stayed despite the threats to their safety. Many were to suffer terribly at the hands of the new regime, as Maj Ali recalls. A typical 'Shah's Pilot' – the name applied by the clerics to those trained during the 1970s – he explained:

The first two F-14As delivered to Iran – BuNos 160299 and 160300, with IIAF titles and Iranian markings already applied – are seen shortly after their arrival at Khatami TFB 8 on 24 January 1976. The first aircraft was flown by a Grumman test pilot and an unknown Iranian RIO while the second jet was crewed by the IIAF's Maj Farvahar and Hughes RIO E S Holmberg (*Grumman via authors*)

'I'd been warned by a very close friend that it was no longer safe for me or my family to stay in Iran. But I didn't believe in my heart that such things could ever be possible in my country. I was soon to become a believer. I was arrested at gun-point in my home by four thugs in front of my family and the same close friend who had warned me to leave Iran. I was jailed, accused of corruption and tortured severely. Today, I'm sure that those pilots who fled Iran made the correct decision. Very few pilots were safe from the powers that reigned in Iran at the time.'

Maj Rassi recalled the experiences of another top Iranian F-14 pilot:

'This officer was trained in America and Israel before the

revolution, and was known for his loyalty to the Shah, which he refused to conceal either during or after the revolution. He never showed himself ready to belong to Khomeyni's "mostazafins", and allowed himself to be arrested by the new regime. Jailed in 1980 when the purging of middle ranks was initiated, he was tortured in prison. He would not have lived longer than October or November 1980 were it not for the Iraqi invasion.

'Once the war had started, he was released from prison – but only after "spiritual rehabilitation" and a reduction in rank – because he was

In order to commemorate the 50th anniversary of the Pahlavi Dynasty, TFB 8 staged a special display at Khatami in 1977. At the time, there were only 21 F-14As in Iran, but 20 were put on display – 11 on the flight line (including 3-6003, 3-6006, 3-6011, 3-6013, 3-6015 and 3-6016), nine of which participated in the fly-past, two in company with a Boeing KC 707-3J9C tanker. Note that even the jets' support equipment – including the starter-cart, seen in the middle foreground to the right – is of US origin (*Grumman*)

known for his skill as a Tomcat pilot. Yet barely a year later he was arrested again, and this time the Revolutionary Guards showed their gratitude for his feats in the war by sentencing him to death once again. The government then decided to rehabilitate him and return him to his unit, but not before he had endured a month of "rehabilitating beatings" by the Guards. It is hard to imagine what the pilots and other officers went through during this period, and I can assure you that only those with the highest physical and mental fortitude survived. And only the strongest managed to recover from their experiences.

'Once out of jail and returned to his unit, this pilot was only permitted to fly with a Weapons System Officer indoctrinated by the regime. Most of these were actually young second lieutenants whose training was discontinued by the 1979 revolution. Few were fully qualified officers, let alone fully qualified fast jet pilots, yet they gave orders to the pilots and ensured their obedience. Nevertheless, this officer never became obedient despite prison, torture and the constant threat of execution. He always remained a "Shah's Pilot", and a true Iranian patriot. He was to become one of the most successful of our Tomcat fliers, and it must be said that the F-14 was in his blood. Sadly, because of the political circumstances, he's also certain to become one of Iran's many "forgotten warriors".'

Maj Ali explained that it was not only aircrew who left Iran in 1978–79, or suffered at the hands of the new regime:

'When the Americans left, many of our best technicians went with them. Others were jailed and several murdered by the new regime. This left us with 80 technicians to maintain a fleet of 77 F-14As. Even then, some were not fully qualified, or had not completed their training.'

By February 1979, training on the F-14 had stopped both in the USA and Iran. To make matters worse, the Americans now tried to sabotage the F-14As and AIM-54s they had to leave behind, as Capt Javad recalled:

'Hughes technicians sabotaged 16 AIM-54s at Khatami before departing for the USA. These 16 Phoenix missiles were ready-to-use live rounds, held at a high state of readiness near the hardened aircraft shelter housing the alert Tomcats. It was later explained in the press that they had sabotaged our whole F-14 fleet, and that we could not use AIM-54s any more. In fact, all the other missiles were safe in their sealed storage/ transport cases, closely guarded in underground bunkers at Khatami. Ironically, we later repaired all 16 damaged rounds using parts stolen from the US Navy.'

Despite these bogus sabotage reports, the US Navy knew exactly what had happened, and soon after the Shah's demise, its Naval Test Center at Point Mugu, California, was assigned a series of top-priority tasks. It was instructed to develop electronic countermeasures aimed at defeating the AIM-54A systems sold to Iran, and to ensure that US AIM-54s would be invulnerable to Iranian electronic countermeasures. The test center was also told to modify the F-14's ICWD radar warning devices to detect emissions from Iranian AWG-9 radars at extreme range.

From the start of the Tomcat programme, the US Navy had never invested additional funds on upgrades. However, with the fall of the Shah, it was now apparently prepared to spend $200 million on these two projects alone. In addition, it pushed hard for a new and upgraded version of the Phoenix (the AIM-54B), which was rushed into service with such haste in the early 1980s that many rounds suffered from poor build quality. Navy admirals knew that such precautions were necessary, as the threat posed by Iranian F-14s in the Persian Gulf was a serious one.

Now the Tomcat became a matter of controversy in Iran as well as in America. For most of 1979 and a good part of 1980, there were low-intensity negotiations held between US officials and the Iranian government concerning the buying back of IRIAF Tomcats. The jets would be refurbished and put back into service with the US Navy or even the USAF, or perhaps sold on to the UK or Saudi Arabia. Most of the Iranian F-14 fleet was grounded at the time while the new regime and surviving air force commanders held a series of meetings to determine the future of the sophisticated and costly interceptors.

Several top officials, including Ayatollah Khomeini's son-in-law, Sadeq Tabatabaie, and Lt Gen Fallahi opted for selling all the F-14s back to the USA. Others, including the CO of the newly re-named Islamic Republic of Iran Air Force, Lt Gen Fakouri, opposed the idea. The matter finally reached the US Congress but was halted when relations between the two countries cooled in the wake of the occupation of the US embassy. Due to the ensuing tensions, the F-14As were slowly returned to service in Iran.

This was done in complete secrecy to avoid revealing the true capabilities of the 'new' IRIAF. For example, the USAF's RH-53D helicopters left behind in the wake of the failed hostage rescue attempt of 30 April 1980 were officially said to have been strafed and destroyed by Iranian Phantom IIs. They were actually hit by two F-14s which had been ordered to attack by Gen Bagheri, then IRIAF CO. He was arrested and executed for alleged cooperation with the Americans because of this order. The official cover-up of the Tomcat's Iranian service had begun.

BuNo 160378 was the 80th and last F-14A built for Iran. The aircraft was held in the USA and scheduled for conversion to the USAF style boom-and-receptacle in-flight refuelling system. In the end it was neither converted nor delivered. When the Shah was overthrown, the jet was put into storage at AMARC. In 1986 it was refurbished and brought up to US Navy standard at NADEP North Island, California. The jet was then issued to the Pacific Missile Test Center on 13 November 1987. Later, it was used by the Naval Air Warfare Center and then by the Weapons Test Squadron at Point Mugu, albeit painted in the standard 'ghost grey' Navy livery (*authors' collection*)

FIRST KILLS

O ne of the first lessons learned in every war is that no plan survives contact with the enemy for long. In the case of the F-14A, declared by the US Navy to be a powerful 'fleet defender' and built to confront large formations of Soviet bombers and defend aircraft carriers using long-range air-to-air missiles, this dictum certainly applied to its Iranian service.

When fighting against Libya in 1986 or Iraq in 1991, for example, US Navy Tomcat crews never expected to go 'feet dry' and fly extensive over-land operations. Yet this was part of the job for Iranian pilots, even if the performance of the jet's AWG-9 radar suffered as a result.

The nature of the first air-to-air combat fought – and won – by F-14s was also unexpected. The first skirmishes between Iraq and Iran occurred on 4 September 1980. Immediately afterwards, the IRIAF started returning an increasing number of F-14s to service. Most of the 77 surviving airframes were not operational, or at least had non-functioning AWG-9s, while their crews lacked fresh training and experience. As a result of non-functioning radar and 'green' crews, F-14 units had come to rely heavily on ground control when it came to intercepting Iraqi aircraft. This soon changed with the escalation of hostilities, as both Tomcat and AWG-9 reliability improved and confidence grew with the flying of more sorties, thus helping crews to recall their training.

Within a few days of the first clashes with the Iraqis, a dozen or so F-14s were back in service flying combat air patrols (CAPs) along the border. On the afternoon of 7 September, five Mil Mi-25 attack helicopters of the 1st Combat Transport Helicopter Squadron, 4th Composite Wing, Iraqi Army Air Corps (IrAAC), penetrated Iranian airspace and attacked several border posts in the Zain al-Qaws region. Their appearance was detected by the local IRIAF radar station, and two F-14As were vectored to intercept.

A few minutes later, the lead Tomcat pilot acquired the Mi-25s on his radar and dived at high speed after them. Uncaging one of his Sidewinders, the pilot attempted a lock-on against the heat of the ground. The AIM-9P Sidewinders were definitely a huge improvement over the AIM-9B/Es of the Vietnam era, but they were not that good. The first missile lost lock-on and flew into the ground behind the rearmost Iraqi. Turning around at a high speed so as to deny the Mi-25s an opportunity to return fire, the Iranian pilot launched another Sidewinder. Again, the missile failed to track and hit the ground. Technically, the engagement should have now been over.

According to modern rules of engagement, and most tactical

War with Iraq did not come as a complete surprise to the IRIAF's F-14 community. Warned by the Americans and Israelis of an impending invasion, Iranian President Bani-Sadr had already ordered several F-14s to be reactivated when relations with the United States became tense in April–May 1980. By 7 September a small number of Tomcats were operational at Khatami air base, and it was one of these aircraft which was to score the type's first kill when its pilot used his 20 mm cannon to claim a Mil Mi-25 attack helicopter of the 1st Combat Transport Helicopter Squadron, IrAAC (*authors' collection*)

Col Hassan Sadeghi was one of Iran's first Tomcat pilots. The revolution and subsequent anarchy caused considerable difficulties for men such as Sadeghi, and many of his contemporaries – both aircrew and technicians – left the country, while others were imprisoned, tortured or even executed. But most were able to return to frontline flying once Iraq invaded Iran in September 1980, and their knowledge and experience was to guarantee a high rate of success for the Tomcat fleet throughout the war (*IIAF Association via authors*)

The first AIM-54A kill was scored by Maj Mohamad-Reza Attaie on 13 September when he shot down an Iraqi MiG-23MS. It followed a decision to grant TFB 8 commanders permission to use the Tomcat and Phoenix in combat to demonstrate their effectiveness to the clerical leadership in Tehran, which was considering selling the whole Tomcat fleet at that time. The wrecked MiG crashed just a few kilometres inside the Iranian border (*authors' collection*)

By early September 1980 enough Tomcats had been made operational to establish permanent CAP stations along the Iraqi border. Several air combats followed shortly afterwards, and the first of these, on 10 September, resulted in the destruction of an IrAF MiG-21RF. The wreckage of the latter is seen here being picked over by an Iranian soldier. Note the substantial remains of the reconnaissance fighter's primary defensive armament, the R-13 (AA-2 'Atoll') air-to-air missile. This R-13 was put on public display in Tehran and variously described as 'proof that the Iraqis use American-built Sidewinder missiles', or as 'remnants of an Iraqi surface-to-surface' rocket! Given the quality of this reporting by the government-controlled Iranian press, it is hardly surprising that the IRIAF's use of the F-14 has been misunderstood by the international media over the past two decades (*authors' collection*)

manuals, an expensive interceptor like an F-14 is not expected to engage a heavily armed helicopter in combat at close quarters. But the Iranian pilot did not hesitate. Selecting 'GUN' on his control column, he put the gunsight pipper over the rearmost Mi-25 and opened fire. The aircraft's M61A1 Vulcan gun spewed out 400 rounds. Many found their mark and the Iraqi attack helicopter exploded in a brilliant ball of fire.

It was therefore an Iranian F-14A which scored the type's first kill almost a year before the US Navy achieved this feat. The weapon used was unexpected, too. Navy legend maintains that a few older F-14 pilots promised to erect a monument to the first individual to score a gun kill in combat. It is unlikely, however, that the pilot who downed the Mi-25 that September afternoon in 1980 will ever reveal his name in public.

The next Tomcat 'first' was much better planned. On 13 September, after more border skirmishes, IRIAF High Command authorised the 81st TFS at TFB 8 to use AIM-54s in combat. An F-14A flown by Maj Mohammad-Reza Attaie (later to command the Esfahan Aerial Region and become a lieutenant general) was assigned to patrol an area over which Iraqi reconnaissance aircraft had been especially active in previous days.

After spending some time on his assigned CAP station, Attaie finally found a suitable target – he shot down a MiG-23MS. Remaining on station for too long, however, he almost ran out of fuel and was forced to make an emergency landing at Omidiyeh air base (TFB 4) in southern Khuzestan. For reasons that still remain unknown, TFB 8 CO Maj Abbas Babaie – who was already notorious for his merciless treatment of pilots and officers considered 'disloyal' to the new regime – ordered Maj Jalal

23

Zandi to bring the F-14 back to base. Zandi had once been a under death sentence passed by the Mullahs, and had only recently been released from prison. Now he was expected to fly to Omidiyeh aboard a Beech Bonanza and bring the F-14 back to a base deeper within Iran. But Zandi disobeyed this order, again for reasons known only to himself – and was imprisoned once again. He was later allowed to return to his unit.

In the days prior to the Iraqi invasion of Iran on 22 September, further F-14s were slowly brought back to operational status. Yet none were in the air when Iraqi fighter bombers attacked Iranian airfields and bases on the afternoon of the 22nd. Instead, the war started a day later for IRIAF Tomcat pilots when they escorted several KC 707s to the Iraqi border to support some of the 120 F-4s that had been sent to strike targets in Iraq.

While on station near Susangerd, a pair of F-14As led by Capt Ali Azimi detected a reconnaissance-configured MiG-21RF escorted by two MiG-23s. Two AIM-54s were fired, one of which blotted out the MiG-21. The fate of the second missile remains unknown, as Azimi's Tomcat subsequently suffered a radar failure.

On the 24th the F-14 crews participated in numerous air combats which saw them claim a total of six kills against Iraqi MiG-21s, MiG-23s and Su-20/22s. Three of these were destroyed in the Ilam region, while another fell near Nakhjir radar station, the fifth in the Salehabad region and the sixth near Malekshahi. The following morning Tomcat crews also helped two damaged Phantom IIs escape Iraqi airspace by flying towards Baghdad and downing two MiG-23s and a MiG-21 near the Iraqi capital.

Capt Javad, who was involved in these early actions, recalled:

'It was clear to any Iranian pilot who flew over the frontlines that there was a war going on. There was little on the ground to stop the massed Iraqi Army from rolling east. However, just as they would soon find out that the Iranian Army would stand its ground and fight, the IrAF was now about to learn that the IRIAF was there to fight too. Our air force intercepted Iraqi fighters over the border, bombed the Iraqis on the ground and launched air strikes deep into enemy airspace.

'By 1300 hrs on 24 September, six F-14As of the 81st TFS were armed and ready for take-off at Khatami air base. IRIAF High Command ordered four of them to join a KC 707 and patrol over northern Iran. The aim was to prevent IrAF bombers from hitting Mehrabad again. I was to fly one of the remaining two Tomcats to patrol the border in the south. There were no AIM-54s available for combat on that mission, and this was not a big deal as there were only two or three qualified crews flying in any case. Only later in the day were two F-14s to fly a mission armed with

F-14A 3-6068, operated by TFB 7, refuels from an Iranian KC 707. Such a capability became important to the success of the Tomcat in Iran, enabling patrol time and combat radius to be increased. Aircraft were able to remain on their CAP stations for up to 12 hours with tanking, or operate deep into Iraq, as during Operation *Sultan Ten* on 29 October 1980. Aerial refuelling also facilitated operations over extended periods at high speeds when F-14s were sent to intercept Soviet MiG-25s that had entered Iranian airspace. Amazingly, after the fall of the Shah in early 1979, Western observers – influenced by the chaos in Iran and the withdrawal of American technical assistance – declared the entire Iranian F-14 fleet to be non-operational. During the autumn of 1980, the IRIAF conducted intense day and night in-flight refuelling training for its Tomcat crews, while simultaneously fighting the IrAF over the Khuzestan front. Although most Iranian F-14 pilots had extensive experience flying F-4s, and had conducted in-flight refuelling as a matter of course during the 1970s, most had to re-qualify after being grounded for much of 1979, and spending the better part of 1980 in prison. Aside from aerial refuelling, the range of IRIAF Tomcats was also boosted in the final years of the war by the secret development of external fuel tanks which were identical to those in service with the US Navy (*authors' collection*)

Phoenix, and they shot down a MiG-21 and frightened the life out of four MiG-23 pilots.

'As we took off there were many reports on the radio of Iraqi aeroplanes crossing into Iran. We detected none, however. Indeed, all we saw were friendly F-5s from TFB 4's 41st, 42nd and 43rd TFSs and F-4s from the 31st, 32nd and 33rd TFSs, which were bombing Iraqi troops with napalm. I ordered the radio reports that we were receiving to be ignored, as we were burning up too much fuel trying to chase down the Iraqi "phantoms". From that point on in the mission we would rely on the information from our own AWG-9s.

'Some 40 minutes after we reached our CAP station 18 km (11 miles) west of Vahdati, my wingman called out, "Multiple bogies detected 23 km (14 miles) to the south-east and closing". Using our AWG-9s and "Combat Tree", we determined that there were four Su-22s and four MiG-21s well within our range. We descended to 20,000 ft, closed to 12 km (seven miles) and locked-up. Each of us fired one AIM-7E, and my Sparrow hit an Iraqi MiG-21 head-on. There was no evasive action. Apparently, the pilot was not aware of the attack. My wingman's missile failed to track, so I ordered him to stay close as we dropped to engage the rest of the Iraqi formation, which was turning west at high speed. My RIO took great pleasure in informing me that the Iraqis were running

Although of poor quality, this unique still taken from the TISEO (Target-Identification System, Electro-Optical) telescopic camera system of an IRIAF 71st TFS F-4E shows an IrAF MiG-23 at the very moment that an AIM-54 warhead exploded just a few metres away from it. The missile was fired on 25 September 1980 by Maj S Naghdi of the 72nd TFS. His F-14A was flying at a height of 6000 m (19,700 ft) at the time, and was just 8000 m (26,250 ft) away from the MiG when the Phoenix was fired against the quickly closing and violently manoeuvring target. During the same combat one of the Phantom IIs shot down a second MiG-23 with a Sparrow fired from a range of 5000 m (16,400 ft). Both MiGs crashed due west of Bandar-e-Khomeini (*authors' collection*)

away. I concluded, "Our reputation must have preceded us!" Not a second later, two MiG-21s turned back into us. These Iraqi pilots were not cowards.

'I switched on "HEAT" for my AIM-9 missiles and rolled left in an effort to get behind and above the enemy. The Iraqis would have none of it. They started climbing, rolling hard to keep us in sight and come out behind our position. But they were too late to save themselves, or so I thought. Our two Tomcats were now at maximum power. I pulled our favourite high AOA manoeuvre and pointed the nose of my F-14A at the rearmost MiG-21, getting a good tone. We were now below 15,000 ft and descending. Just as I fired a Sidewinder, my wingman came over the radio screaming, "ENGINE STALL!"

'My Sidewinder hit the MiG, but any joy I felt was now replaced by urgent concern for my wingman. The F-14's yaw characteristics after the loss of an engine at low altitude and high AOA are not good. My wingman, himself just short of launching a Sidewinder at the other MiG, was now using all his skill to keep his Tomcat flying. To make matters worse, we then lost sight of the other MiG. There was little I could do without relocating him. After what seemed like an age, but was actually only a few seconds, we detected him on our radar running away – he was most likely low on fuel.

'When my wingman's right engine stalled he was at a height of 10,000 ft at maximum dry power, with his speed at almost 520 knots and his nose at 45 degrees AOA. The pilot knew he had only ten seconds to save his aircraft and maybe even his life, and that of his RIO. He later said, "I had increased my airspeed to close on the lead MiG just as you were firing a missile at the rear one. I was getting a tone from the AIM-9 in my headset, so I didn't hear the engine stall warning. I did see the warning light next to my HUD, however, and not a moment too soon. I literally stopped breathing then and immediately shut the stalling engine down, while pulling the stick all the way back and holding it there.

'"My F-14 pitched up to between 70 and 75 degrees AOA and developed a yaw rate of 44 to 46 degrees per second to the right side, with my airspeed dropping off to 82 knots. I initiated recovery, the aeroplane responded well and ten seconds later we were flying level on one engine, with my heart racing at 10,000 beats per second. My RIO was scanning the skies as if nothing had happened!"

'During the post-flight inspection, we found out that the mid-compression bypass valves had remained closed on one of the engines, shutting it down during the climb. Normally, this valve opens at high AOA to improve engine stall margin, and you lose up to 14 per cent of engine thrust. However, this time it failed. We had some luck on this mission as both crews survived. They were to fly many more times, and show the Iraqis they couldn't operate freely – or without cost – over Iran.'

DIRECT INVOLVEMENT

Throughout October, F-14 crews fought a series of air battle with Iraqi fighters, scoring at least 25 confirmed kills mainly against MiG-23BNs. But other types were also encountered, as Capt Nuzran relates:

'By October 1980, the war between Iraq and Iran was in full swing, and there was no turning back. We had our orders – Iraq would be defeated and their leaders destroyed by the Iranian military, or we would all become part of the revolutionary martyrdom. The IRIAF was now on a full war footing, and we were to hold nothing back in our efforts to repel the Iraqi Army from Iranian territory. But we were spread very thinly.

'The general order for IRIAF F-4 units was to destroy all Iraqi oil terminals in the Persian Gulf and maintain control of the Straits of Hormuz in cooperation with the Navy. Simultaneously, F-4 and F-5 units were also tasked with stopping two powerful Iraqi Army drives deep into Iran, while Phantom IIs had to strike strategic targets mainly in the Baghdad area. The Tomcat community was to get its orders too.

'The southern port of Khoramshahr was surrounded and then captured by Iraqi forces. Abadan was besieged and under daily attack by the IrAF, with bombing strikes killing many defenders. So, on 19 October, President Bani-Sadr ordered 81st TFS Tomcats to become directly involved in the defence of Abadan until other IRIAF units could be pulled from the strategic air war with Iraq.

'The 81st was operating at far from full strength, but we would have dedicated tanker support. We calculated that we could sustain three or four days of intensive operations over the city before having to stand down. At 0600 hrs on 20 October we started flying CAPs over Abadan, keeping two F-14s permanently on station. At around 0920 hrs, the two Tomcats led by Capt M Hashem All-e-Agha – TFB 8's deputy CO for Operations – detected the first two Iraqi jets approaching from the north some 34 km (21 miles) from Abadan. The F-14s turned to intercept.

'Moving up from the south, they closed on what was now clearly two pairs of MiG-21s. All-e-Agha ordered his wingman to take the southern pair, while he himself went for the northern jets. From a range of 12 km (seven miles) All-e-Agha fired the first AIM-7 but it fell away harmlessly. His RIO then locked-on with another Sparrow and the pilot fired. The missile flew straight into the lead Iraqi MiG-21, destroying it with a direct hit. His wingman, meanwhile, had suffered guidance data-link problems and had to watch as two of his Sparrows flew off unguided into the skies. Nevertheless, the MiGs had had enough and turned away from Abadan.

'The Iraqis returned two days later, and this time a pair of MiG-23s was intercepted by two F-14s – one jet was shot down by an AIM-9 fired from very close range. On the 25th, four Su-22s were intercepted by our Tomcats and one was shot down by a Sidewinder and a second damaged by a Sparrow. Another engagement followed on 26 October. After some hard manoeuvring, an Iraqi MiG-21 was shot down by an AIM-9P but the Tomcat flew into the debris and was damaged. The 81st now had to stand down in order to give its crews some rest and allow urgent maintenance to be carried out on its aircraft.'

THE *SULTAN* STRIKE

There was no respite for the IRIAF F-14s, however. As more and more pilots and groundcrew were released from prison, a greater number of Tomcats became operational and more sorties were flown. In late October, after the capture of Khoramshahr, the Iraqi Army started new offensive operations. To many observers it appeared as if the massed Iraqi units would easily overcome the disorganised Iranian Army and Revolutionary Guards.

Maj Abbas Hazin became one of the early IRIAF F-14 heroes following his encounter with two MiG-21s from Qaleh Saleh air base over Shahid Asyaee, north-east of Ahwazhe, on 26 October 1980. Flying with RIO Capt Khosrow Ekhbari (one of the IRIAF's best F-4 pilot/WSOs, who was subsequently killed on 4 February 1981), Hazin fired a Sidewinder from minimum range and saw his target explode in flames. Unable to avoid debris from the target due to its close proximity, Hazin felt his aircraft shudder as its left wing was struck by several large chunks of wreckage. Both the AIM-7 and AIM-9 mounted on the wing shoulder pylon were ripped off, and further MIG debris was ingested into the port engine. Black soot from the exploding jet also covered the F-14. Struggling to keep his damaged aircraft in the air, Hazin managed to coax the Tomcat some 400 km (250 miles) back to Khatami, where he landed safely. He was awarded the Fat'h Medal for his actions on this day. Abbas Hazin rose to the rank of lieutenant general, but died of heart failure on 29 November 2000 while serving as CO of the 'Shahid Babaie' Aerial District of Esfahan (*authors' collection*)

However, the Iranians were already bolstering their defences, and putting up unexpectedly fierce resistance against which the rigid Iraqi tactics proved unsuccessful. IRIAF interceptors also established air superiority over the battlefield, making it impossible for the IrAF and the Iraqi artillery to support ground units without suffering losses. Maj Ali and Capt Javad remember:

'After we established air superiority over the front, the IRIAF – reinforced by additional "Shah's pilots" released from jail – took the opportunity to increase the number of Battlefield Air Interdiction and Close Air Support sorties being flown. Also, under the IRIAF's protection, and with the help of the IRIAA, our army was able to move ground units forward to the front. This finally offset the Iraqis' initial numerical advantage.

'But in response, the Iraqi regime ordered the remnants of the IrAF to target Iranian cities, killing innocent civilians. They also started firing SS-1B/C Scud and LUNA/FROG-7 ballistic missiles at our urban areas. These attacks got so bad that Ayatollah Khomeini had to support President Bani-Sadr's decision to release even more jailed Iranian pilots. Khomeini soon ordered the IRIAF to increase the scope of its offensive deep into Iraq, sometimes even selecting targets himself. We had no tactical ballistic missiles, but we did have American-made Phantom IIs and Tomcats, and these were much better at hitting key targets with precision than anything the Iraqis had.

'In mid October 1980 the commanders at TFB 1 obtained very precise intelligence about the deployment of 47 French Air Force technicians and several Mirage F 1C fighters to al-Hurriyah air base near Mosul, in northern Iraq. They were there to help train Iraqi pilots converting onto the Mirage F 1EQs ordered in 1977 and now ready for collection in France.

'Of course, we were keen to stop the Iraqis training on these aircraft, and we also wanted to "welcome" the French to the war. Consequently, a plan for the first IRIAF strike deep into Iraq – Operation *Sultan Ten* – was devised. The key people behind this plan, which called for a sizeable force of F-4s, escorted by F-14s, to fly over 300 km (187 miles) into northern Iraq, were Col J Afshar and Maj H Shoghi.

'We were informed at our briefing by Col Afshar that the plan called for a total of six F-4Es from the 32nd and the 33rd TFSs – each loaded with 12 Mk 82 bombs – to attack Mosul, approaching from the north instead of the east. This would allow all of our aeroplanes to bypass 12 of the 16 known Iraqi SA-2, SA-3 and SA-6 SAM batteries south and east of Mosul, plus two known IrAF MiG-21 CAPs which often patrolled to the east of the city. However, our Phantom IIs were so heavy with bombs that they would need inflight refuelling to get home, so two IRIAF tankers from TFB 1 were assigned to fly with them deep into Iraq. These would in turn be protected by two F-14As from the 81st TFS. This mission was one of the few times during the war that our KC 707 tankers and F-14As were officially permitted to enter Iraqi airspace.

'To ensure that the Iraqis, and their French friends, would be surprised by our attack, strike aircraft of the *Sultan* formation, together with tankers, would penetrate Iraqi airspace after crossing Turkey. This was not the last operation in which we used Turkish airspace.

'Col Afshar told us that for this mission we were to concentrate on the "basics". F-4 pilots were to keep each other in sight, find the Iraqi targets and bomb them. Then he addressed the escorting Tomcat pilots, informing us that, "Our mission requires that your fighters stay with the tankers, for if both tankers are lost, everything is lost."

'Afshar would command the operation from one of the tankers ("Sultan 9"), and his last orders before he dismissed us were, "Keep quiet about the mission, and keep quiet on the radio." Three tankers (one spare), eight Phantom IIs (two spares) and three F-14As (one spare) took off from TFB 2, near Tabriz, just before dawn on 29 October. We joined up just south of Orumiyeh, using the Zagros mountains to hide from Iraqi early warning radars – many Iraqi radars could see deep into our airspace. Just before crossing into Turkey, our extra (third) tanker topped off all the *Sultan* package fighters and turned back, escorted by the spare F-4Es and F-14A. We maintained radio silence, and continued to do so for most of the mission.

Iranian Tomcats have proven how well they were built by the Grumman 'Ironworks' on numerous occasions. These two photographs illustrate the damage that an engine bay explosion can inflict on an F-14. While refuelling from a KC 707 tanker, the crew heard a loud bang from the right engine compartment and quickly disengaged. They then shut down the damaged engine and headed back to base. By the time the jet landed, it was on fire, with flames trailing some ten to fifteen metres behind the right engine, engulfing the tail section. The explosion had caused severe damage to the right engine intake, bleed doors and ramps, and had blocked the passage of air to the engine face. The pilot nevertheless made a safe emergency landing (*authors' collection*)

'As our group flew north, we crossed into Turkey, using the Yuk Pass to hide our progress. The Turks had us on their radars at least once but chose to do nothing. Upon leaving Turkish airspace, we then entered Iraq – undetected – using the Amadi Pass within the Jabel Sinjar Mountains. We all refuelled once again, before the Phantom IIs dropped down towards the target, passing between the Iraqi cities of Dahuk and Aqrah.

'The two tankers remained in orbit at low level – burning lots of fuel – over the Dahuk plains, closely watched over by two F-14As, which took turns in activating their powerful AWG-9 radars and refuelling while waiting for the Phantom IIs.

'The strike package was led by Maj H Shoghi ("Sultan 1"). A brave leader and accurate strike pilot, he approached the target with little problem. Many hits were scored and al-Hurriyah air base was left in a chaos of smoke and fire. We felt that this time luck was truly on our side. But then our Tomcats detected four suspected Iraqi interceptors only 70 km (44 miles) south of the tankers, and flying into an area between them and the Phantom IIs.

'Using the "Combat Tree" equipment and RWRs, the Tomcat crews determined that their foes were four MiG-23s – most likely MiG-23MFs from Qayyarah West air base, where we knew the Iraqis had stationed their first squadron equipped with this type, as well as 16 MiG-21s. Col Afshar was informed, and he did a few fast calculations, determining that within the next ten to fifteen minutes the MiGs would run out of fuel and be forced to return to their base. While they were doing so, they would fly head-on into our Phantom IIs as the latter, also short of fuel, tried to reach the tankers.

'Under normal circumstances, our Phantom II pilots would have had little problem in destroying the MiGs. However, on this mission, fuel was life, and the F-4 crews' ability to reach the tankers undisturbed and without any detour was crucial, as they carried no air-to-air missiles. Col Afshar acted swiftly. He ordered F-14A "Sultan 7", piloted by Capt K Sedghi, and his wingman ("Sultan 8", flown by Capt M Taibbe) to intercept the MiG-23s and destroy them before they encountered the Phantom IIs.

'There was no time to waste. Without hesitation, the Tomcats joined formation and turned south, climbing to 15,000 ft. Checking their systems, Sedghi and Taibbe concluded that the Iraqis had not detected them, so they continued to climb to 20,000 ft. From this height they would have several attack options. There was no other way to clear the path for the *Sultan* Phantom IIs, and the thought of leaving the six crews to run out of fuel and eject over Iraq was simply unacceptable.

'The two F-14s joined up in a combat spread – a very flexible, mutual-support formation developed by the US Navy which worked far better than those normally used by our F-4 squadrons. It allowed freedom of action during both the intercept and ensuing air combat phases of the engagement. Whichever Tomcat gets the first radar or visual contact has the tactical lead, and can run the flight for the intercept, but the lead can always be passed on to another F-14 if necessary. Such tactics were never used in our F-4 and F-5 units. There, the flight leader remained in charge, and gave all the orders.

'"Sultan 7" was armed with two AIM-54As, three AIM-7s and two AIM-9s, while "Sultan 8" was loaded with six AIM-7s and two AIM-9s.

A somewhat dusty front cockpit of an Iranian F-14A, photographed in 1980. At that time there were few differences between the cockpits (front and back) of an IRIAF Tomcat and a standard US Navy F-14, other than the presence of more sensitive avionics in the latter aircraft which had been hastily installed to counter the Western-built systems featured in the Iranian F-14s (*authors' collection*)

The two Tomcats thus had longer-ranged weapons and better combat persistence than the four MiGs. Yet their success depended on not giving away their presence too early, and certainly not causing the IrAF to scramble even more interceptors until the *Sultan* Phantom IIs could be refuelled and the whole Iranian package safely escorted out of Iraqi airspace.

'As they continued climbing to 22,000 ft, Capt Sedghi's RIO quickly ran down his checklist for all rear cockpit equipment as he got ready for combat. All armament (except for Sidewinders and guns), sensor controls and keyboard and communication panels are situated on the RIO's left console. The electronic countermeasures and navigational display, as well as the panel for the IFF interrogator, are on the right.

'The RIO operated the AWG-9 in track-while-scan (TWS) mode, keeping contact with all four MiGs as the radar swept across the sky and stored the last known position of the targets in the computer. The latter then estimated their next position. The heading, speed and altitude of the Iraqi MiGs, as well as launch zone priorities, were all determined by the Tomcat's weapons systems. There was only one drawback – the TWS is useful for deploying AIM-54 missiles only, and just two of these were carried, both on "Sultan 7".

'At a range of about 56 km (35 miles) from the Iraqi fighters, Sedghi's AWG-9 mission computer established a track file on them. They were flying in a split formation, made up of two pairs, one behind the other – the leading pair was to be the first target. Sedghi ordered the noise jammers of the two F-14As to be turned on, but his ECM system failed just seconds after it was activated. The one in Taibbe's Tomcat had to cover both aircraft.

'At 33 km (20 miles), Sedghi cleared his RIO to "light off" the AIM-54s when ready – and he was ready! The first AIM-54 was fired and then began to climb towards the Iraqi MiGs, which were cruising at a height of 30,000 ft. Some eight seconds later the second Phoenix followed.

'The MiG pilots continued straight ahead as if on a routine training flight. It was clear that they still had no clue about the closing Tomcats – we knew the MiGs supplied to the Iraqis carried only rudimentary radar and RWRs. As the crews of the two F-14s tracked the progress of the AIM-54s, they received a radio call from "Sultan 9", informing them that the Iraqi MiGs had been alerted to the attack on al-Hurriyah air base, and that they had been ordered to turn west to intercept the Iranian F-4s. The

F-14A 3-6046 (BuNo 160344) is loaded with empty Phoenix pallets and pylons beneath the fuselage and the wing glove, respectively. Iranian F-14As were seldom seen carrying six AIM-54s either before or after the revolution. Pilots deemed such a configuration to be too heavy for dogfighting. The jet's landing speed was also considerably increased. Reluctant to ripple fire missiles at multiple targets, the Iranians reporteldy modified their AWG-9 radars so that they could engage only one target at a time in an effort to reduce wear and tear on the system (*Grumman*)

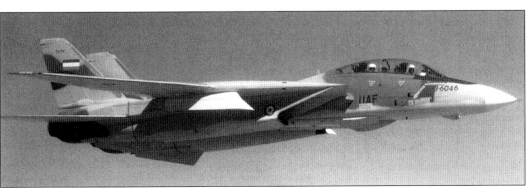

Iraqi MiGs were about to turn, but not yet! Luckily for us the Iraqis never had time to obey their orders.

'The first AIM-54 slammed into the lead MiG-23, blotting it out immediately. Sedghi's RIO simply exclaimed, "The Iraqi bastard is gone!" The second Phoenix, however, appeared to have missed, for the MiG at which it was aimed continued to maintain its course after it should have been hit. Seconds later, however, the RIO noticed that the MiG was actually diving towards the ground at high speed, obviously out of control. "Sultan 8" confirmed the kill, reporting that the AIM-54 must have crippled the second MiG-23 by early or late proximity fuse warhead detonation. In either case, the large warhead did exactly what it was designed to do. Now we had no doubt what a remarkable weapon the F-14A and AIM-54A truly represented.'

'Sultans 7' and '8' had no time to celebrate, for there were still two surviving MiG-23s that posed a threat to the returning Phantom IIs. Obviously in confusion, the Iraqis first turned slowly to the south, then east and then started descending. They had no clue about what had hit them, nor from which side. Sedghi and Taibbe monitored them on their radars, waiting for an opportunity to destroy still more MiGs.

With the sudden demise of the first MiG-23 pair, the surviving pilots had made two grave tactical errors. Firstly, they turned their tails towards the two Tomcats they knew nothing about. And secondly, the Iraqi pilots descended, thus giving the height advantage to their enemy. Sedghi felt very confident as he selected zone five afterburner for a few seconds in order to gain extra speed.

Switching their radars to Pulse-Tracking mode, he and Taibbe started to set up an AIM-7E-4 attack on the two MiGs which were now only 12 km (seven miles) ahead. It was Taibbe's turn to take the lead, and Sedghi climbed 2000 ft away to his right so as to be able to provide him with mutual support by rolling down on any Iraqi fighter that might close undetected. Although the AIM-7E-4 was a much-improved version of the earlier Sparrow missile used in the Vietnam War, it still required good teamwork between pilot and RIO to ensure its effective employment.

Just minutes away from firing, Taibbe called Sedghi. 'Be advised that I have a CSD (computer signal data) warning light now!' The latter, fitted in the F-14's rear cockpit, indicated a failure of the CSD converter, which was used to collate all the Tomcat's various target tracking and missile acquistion avionics. The CSD had to be functioning properly for the jet to be effective in combat, and if the F-14 had suffered such a failure on the ground prior to take off, it would have been scrubbed from the mission.

It took around five minutes to reconfigure the CSD, then some six to eight minutes for the F-14's inertial navigation system to realign itself. But, 'Sultans 7' and '8' were airborne, 300 km (187 miles) inside Iraq and just moments away from engaging two hostile interceptors. Without CSD, 'Sultan 8' had nothing but its gun to defend itself with, and would need considerable luck and a dedicated fighter escort to make it home.

Sedghi called, "Seven" to "Eight" – I will continue. You are to withdraw to orbit area and hold with "Nine" and "Ten" until I come back. "Eight", be advised – use your altitude heading and reference set only as a heading and distance indicator'. 'Sultan 8' responded, '"Seven" to "Eight", I copy. Good hunting', then departed.

Sedghi switched to 'HEAT' to activate one of his Sidewinders and advised his RIO to keep checking their 'six' (immediately behind their jet). The RIO responded that the ECM was down, but that all other systems were operational and the advisory panel was clear. Then the pilot of 'Sultan 7' engaged afterburner once again.

The two MiGs were now down to 10,000 ft, but nothing in the IrAF inventory could out-turn an F-14A at low level. The Tomcat was closing rapidly, and at a distance of 1500 yards Sedghi got the signal that the MiGs were within range of his AIM-9Ps. At that moment the Iraqis suddenly broke formation, their leader banking right and his wingman left – the lone Tomcat had been spotted.

Sedghi turned behind the leader and clung on to his tail, closing on the MiG trying to out-turn him. Seconds later, as the MiG rolled out of the turn and started a climb, he got a good tone and launched the first Sidewinder from very close range. Almost instantaneously the AIM-9 hit the target's tail, causing yellow flames to erupt from the MiG. Fragments then broke off the jet's wing roots as it started its final plunge earthwards. Transfixed by the MiG's demise, Sedghi was jolted back to reality by his RIO. 'Captain. We have a MiG on our "six" and closing fast! Low fuel warning in two minutes!'

At almost 520 mph, low on fuel and with an Iraqi MiG-23 on his tail, Sedghi performed what the Americans call a 'break turn' – he pulled the control column all the way back, then kicked in full rudder to generate a large yaw and roll rate to slow the jet down, using the Tomcat as a foil in a high-pitch position. With the control column still held all the way back, and using full rudder for an inside turn, pulling max g-loads in a slowing speed scissors manoeuvre, the Tomcat's speed dropped down to 150 mph within seconds. The nose of the jet went through the vertical and then dropped down on the MiG-23 as it flashed by at high speed.

Engaging afterburner, Sedghi closed on the Iraqi's tail and got a good tone from his last Sidewinder. The missile hit the MiG's lower tail section, causing the jet to roll over on its back trailing flame and smoke. The Iraqi pilot ejected seconds later.

Keeping Sedghi updated on the fuel state of the Tomcat, his RIO called, 'Captain. We must disengage afterburner and return to the tankers – NOW! We're almost out of fuel!' Replying that he had probably saved them for the second time that day, Sedghi turned 'Sultan 7' around to rejoin the tankers. He said later:

'I told my RIO to keep a close watch for MiGs, but this was just to take his mind off our low fuel state. I'm sure that if I'd asked him about our fuel he'd have told me that there was none left for the flight back to our tankers. He would have been right. I contacted "Sultan 9" and informed him about our situation, learning in return that all the Phantom IIs had returned safely and the whole package was now heading home. Checking the radio, to our great delight and joy we found the tankers only ten miles away hiding behind a mountain ridge. F-4s "Sultans 1" and "3" were escorting a single tanker that had been sent to help us get back to Iran. Fuel is life.'

The F-4s which had hit Mosul had also destroyed two MiG-21s and three Mi-8s helicopters on the ground. At least one French technician had been killed during the raid, while another was wounded. All French personnel were immediately ordered home. Three of the four MiG-23 pilots downed by Sedghi had also been killed – one of the latter was identified as Capt Ahmed Sabah, who had reportedly shot down two IRIAF F-5Es on the first day of the war.

TOMCAT'S LONG CLAWS

On 1 December 1980, Tomcat crews from the 82nd TFS claimed no less than three Iraqi fighters during a single engagement near Abadan. The next morning the same unit was again successful when Capt F Dehghan (also a C-130 pilot with the 1st TTW) was on his CAP station 68 miles west of Bushehr, covering Khark Island as well as the Nowrouz and Cyrus oil rigs. After orbiting for some time, GCI advised Dehghan of multiple bogies inbound from the north, closing fast to a range of 19.5 miles.

The time factor was critical, so Dehghan's RIO worked fast. Lock-on to the first two Iraqi MiG-21s – which were flying cover for trailing Su-20s – was attained when they were only ten miles away. This was close to the minimum engagement range for the Phoenix, but the latter weapon had to be used as the lone F-14 would have otherwise been too heavy to engage the IrAF fighters in close combat.

The RIO selected PSTT (pulse single target track) mode, acquired lock-on and activated one of the weapons under the fuselage. The pilot then fired an AIM-54A in short-range engagement mode, which allowed the active seeker head to activate immediately upon launching. The missile fell away from the jet, its motor ignited and the round acquired the target, flying straight into it. Moments later, a series of large splashes was seen in the water as chunks of MiG-21 fell out of the sky after the fighter had been blown apart by the missile. Having witnessed its demise at close quarters, the rest of the formation turned north and fled at high speed.

In late December, the Iranian Tomcat community was redeployed. F-14As from the 72nd TFS were assigned to the 73rd TFS and sent to Mehrabad, where the detachment became known as the '83rd TFS', even though no such unit was officially organised until after the war. The 72nd TFS was duly re-equipped with F-4Ds, although many of its pilots continued flying both types.

Meanwhile, the crews of the 81st and 82nd TFSs started flying virtually permanent CAPs over the northern Persian Gulf in an effort to defend Iranian oil installations, ports and shipping in the area. With their very long range and far-reaching weapons system, Tomcats on patrol between Bushehr and Khark could attack the Iraqis as soon as they entered the airspace over the northern Persian Gulf. Crews had to rely on their AWG-9 system for target detection, as the performance of the Iranian ground-based radar was well known to the Iraqis, thanks to the Americans having revealed its secrets to them pre-war. This equipment was also obsolescent and unreliable due to a shortage of parts.

On 10 November 1980, four Iraqi MiG-23s were attacking Iranian ground troops north of Abadan when they were intercepted by two F-14s from the 82nd TFS. One MiG was blown apart by an AIM-7 at a height of just 300 m (980 ft), and this photograph was taken of the wreckage as it fell to earth. The remaining three MiGs immediately fled back to Iraq (*authors' collection*)

MiG-21s of various different versions were the main opponents for Iranian Tomcats in the early stages of the war. This particular MiG-21RF (serial 21302) survived these fierce air battles, only to be captured and then destroyed by US troops at Tallil air base, in southern Iraq, in March 1991. Two MiG-21RFs are known to have been shot down by IRIAF F-14As in September 1980 (*authors' collection*)

THREE-TO-ONE

I n November 1980, the pace of operations declined for the first time due to bad weather. Nevertheless, by January 1981 IRIAF F-14A crews are known to have downed at least 33 Iraqi fighters and one helicopter. At least five of these kills were achieved using Phoenix missiles.

On the morning of 7 January 1981, two F-14As were on CAP station between Bushehr and Khark when they were warned by GCI of four MiG-23BNs flying in tight formation towards Ahwaz on an interdiction mission. Employing their AWG-9s to great effect, the Tomcats' radars highlighted all four jets and established a target file for each of them. As usual, the battle was opened by the lead F-14 firing a single AIM-54A – on this occasion from a range of over 50 km (30 miles) – which hit the lead MiG. The jet disintegrated in a huge explosion that was obviously fed by the bombs it was carrying.

To their great surprise, the two Tomcat crews then saw a second MiG-23BN crash, apparently damaged by debris from the leader's jet, followed by a third, which spiralled slowly into the sea. There were rumours within the IRIAF that something similar had happened during an engagement with Iraqi MiG-23s in November or December 1980. But in that case, the F-14 crew had claimed 'only' two MiGs with a single AIM-54. This, however, was the first, and so far only, known case in which a single air-to-air missile had accounted for three enemy fighters. Better still, the fourth MiG-23BN was observed retreating north trailing a plume of smoke. It is not known whether it landed safely or not.

Another Iraqi formation intercepted on 29 January was slightly luckier. It was detected at noon by Iranian ground-based radar flying at only 100 ft. Two 81st TFS F-14As that were on patrol over Bushehr both immediately turned to engage, and the lead RIO established a lock-on. After the IFF interrogator had confirmed the targets as Su-20s, a single AIM-54A was fired from a range of 54 km (33 miles). The large missile soared directly towards the low-flying targets, hitting one of the Sukhois in the centre of the fuselage and cutting it in two. Although the fuse failed to detonate the warhead, the F-14 wingman reported seeing a large fireball crash into the sea. The rest of the Iraqi formation escaped.

Through the rest of the winter and into the spring of 1981, IRIAF F-14s continued flying intensive operations. Most sorties were conducted over the northern Persian Gulf in defence of the crucial oil installations on Khark Island, from which over 90 per cent of Iranian oil exports were shipped.

In October 1980, and again between January and April 1981, Iranian Tomcats were active in the area between the Iraqi city of Basrah and Bandar-e-Khomeini, the northernmost Iranian Persian Gulf port. Their main tasks were to defend ground units along the frontlines between Abadan and Khoramshahr, support the 41st TFW (stationed at Vahdati, to the north of this area), the 51st TFW (at Omidiyeh and Masjed Soleiman) and the 61st TFW (at Bushehr), and escort ship convoys bringing supplies and reinforcements up from Bandar Abbas, in southern Iran (*authors' collection*)

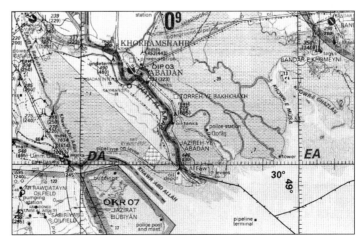

Loaded with four AIM-54s, two AIM-7s and two AIM-9s, F-14A 3-6079 approaches the runway at Mehrabad at the end of yet another CAP mission to the west of Tehran. This war load was routinely seen in the early stages of the conflict with Iraq, but once combat experience proved that two AIM-54s were usually enough to accomplish the task, four of the bulky missiles were rarely carried again. The jet's agility in a dogfight was compromised by the carriage of four Phoenix rounds, but entering a turning fight with two AIM-54s on the fuselage pallets had no effect on the Tomcat whatsoever (*authors' collection*)

Two MiG-23s were shot down in this area on 4 April. Three weeks later, on the 21st, a single F-14 flown by Capt Amir was on a patrol over Khark at 24,000 ft when the RIO detected two inbound MiG-23s. The Iraqis frequently tried to approach Khark when only one F-14 was on CAP, the second jet having headed north to refuel.

Flying at 570 kts at an altitude of 5000 ft, the two MiGs were picked up at a range of just 20 miles (32 km) by the F-14. Seconds later, both jets made a high-speed left turn and disappeared from the radar screen. This was one of the first times that the Iraqis had executed the 'beaming' manoeuvre, turning 90 degrees to the F-14 to break the AWG-9's lock.

This manoeuvre is effective against radars working in pulse-Doppler mode, and it was used by the Iraqis in 1991 when engaging USAF F-15s. Theoretically, the AWG-9 could establish a track file and predict where the target was to re-appear. But in this case the range between the MiGs and the F-14 was so close that there was no time for the processor to compute. Descending to 3000 ft, and accelerating to 600 kts, Capt Amir followed with a turn to the right to initiate combat. He later reported:

'Suddenly, I saw the first MiG at "two o'clock", some five miles (8 km) away, and slightly higher. I looked behind it over my right shoulder to find the wingman, as I was searching for him and not for the leader. I couldn't see him, so I decided to go after the leader. I lit up the 'burner and made a tight turn to position myself behind the MiG. I switched to "GUN" because I was in an ideal position to fire, being only 500 ft behind the MiG-23. I fired several bursts without using my radar to keep his RWR silent – from this distance, the slightest movement of the target could ruin my aim. I expected the MiG to explode, but it continued. Then he became aware of me on his tail and began making smooth turns to the left and right, reducing his altitude and trying to accelerate away.

'My bullets had missed, so I activated the radar for a lock-on. By then the gap between us had opened to something like 1.5 miles (2.5 km), but I was accelerating and was soon almost 180 kts faster than him. I selected "HEAT" and immediately got a very strong tone from the Sidewinder. I pressed the trigger but the missile failed to fire. Time was rapidly running out. I was in the best position to launch at the MiG ahead, but I had another one somewhere behind me, and the missile wouldn't fire. As I glanced over my left wing to see what was going on there, the Sidewinder suddenly jumped off the rail and went straight for the Iraqi MiG. There was no failure – time was passing so slowly for me that the one-second lapse between pressing the trigger and the launch seemed abnormally long.

'When the missile hit the "Flogger" I started a high-g pull-up to the right, looking for the other MiG. Then I felt a slight jolt and several warning lights came on. I broke and positioned myself behind the second

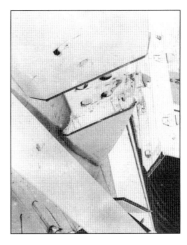

On the morning of 21 April 1981 an IRIAF F-14 left Bushehr air base and headed for a CAP station north of Khark Island. Two bogies were soon detected at low level, flying in close formation, and the patrolling Tomcat dived to engage. However, the two Iraqi jets used the Doppler effect to evade the Tomcat's AWG-9, and the F-14 pilot had to rely on a visual acquisition at just five miles. Spotting two MiG-23s, he rapidly sent an AIM-9 up the lead fighter's jetpipe. However, the wingman had also fired a heat-seeking missile at the F-14, and it peppered the jet's left engine and fuselage with shrapnel. Despite extensive damage to both TF30s, the Tomcat remained controllable and returned to base to be repaired (*authors' collection*)

Soon after the start of the war, it became clear to the IRIAF that available stocks of spares would not last long, and that it could not depend on the unreliable black market to keep its F-14s operational. Consequently, great efforts were made to produce spares locally, and thus become self-reliant in maintaining the F-14s. In 1982, Iran Aircraft Industries (IACI), in cooperation with the so-called 'Self-sufficiency Jihad' group of the IRIAF and various Iranian universities, and with clandestine US and Israeli support, managed to produce simpler spare parts like tyres and brake discs. Over the following years more advanced capabilities were developed. Aircraft 3-6003 is seen here undergoing a complex overhaul at IACI's Mehrabad works (*authors' collection*)

Iraqi, while selecting "GUN" again. It didn't work. I resorted to "HEAT", but that wouldn't work either. My Tomcat was at 2300 ft and 580 kts at that time. Only then did I notice AAA rounds exploding around us. I realised what I thought was the second MiG was actually a plume from the AAA explosions. In fact, the enemy jet was still somewhere behind us, and had already fired two missiles. My RIO had made several attempts to warn me but I was so preoccupied with the imaginary target that I didn't hear him. I unloaded and disengaged.

'After landing, we inspected the damage. The blades on the left engine had intermingled, the right engine was also damaged and the fuselage was riddled with shrapnel. Obviously there had been a large explosion under my Tomcat!'

The F-14s continued engaging the IrAF at regular intervals during the second half of 1981, with crews flying hundreds of combat sorties, many of which lasted for over six hours and involved several in-flight refuellings. Maj Ali summarised the effort to keep the jets operational:

'During the war we tried to maintain 60 F-14s in operational condition. At first, we more or less managed that, but on average we usually kept between 40 and 45 Tomcats combat ready. This was by no means easy. The primary maintenance facilities were at Mehrabad, where the bulk of the spares and most of our technicians – initially a total of only

On 14 April 1981, the F-14 flown by Capt Jafar Mardani, seen here, and 1Lt Gholam-Hossein Abdolshahi, crashed near Bushehr. Both crewmen were killed, and there have been contradictory reports about the cause of their demise ever since. While some suggested a flat-spin, IRIAF investigation determined that a MIM-23 HAWK SAM was responsible (*authors' collection*)

11 officers and 33 NCOs – were based. This concentrated resources for overhaul and depot-level maintenance, but it proved to be a futile effort.

'Having only a few people and aircraft at Mehrabad did very little for the maintenance of the whole fleet, the bulk of which was based at Khatami. Soon enough, the IRIAF issued a call to the nation's best engineers and scientists to help maintain our F-14s. Many former IIAF maintenance people were also released from jail to offer additional help.

'Spares were also a problem. In 1979 the US government had held back several highly important shipments. At great cost, we kept a small trickle of spare parts coming in using third-party arms dealers to buy equipment through Israel. Such an arrangement was necessary to allow Khomeini's people to deny any dealings with his sworn enemy, the "Zionist entity". The Israelis, however, not only charged high prices, but were also unable to supply many of the parts we needed as they had no F-14s. We also received technical assistance from Israel – instructions on how to repair certain items, particularly electronics. Most of this came in the form of instructions written by the Israeli Defence Force's Foreign Service Office, led by Yitzhak Rabin. His cooperation ended in late 1983.'

Despite continued success in combat in 1981, the Tomcat fleet also suffered its first known loss of the war on 14 April 1981 when the F-14A flown by Capt Jafar Mardani and 1Lt Gholam-Hossein Abdolshahi crashed into the Persian Gulf – both men were killed. The exact cause of their demise remains unclear. Mardani was apparently in the middle of aerial refuelling when IrAF fighters were reported in the area. According to one account, he made a sudden breakaway from the tanker, causing the jet to break up and explode. Another report suggests that he went into a flat spin while disengaging from the tanker and was unable to recover.

According to IRIAF sources, the Tomcat was shot down in the Bushehr area by a 'friendly' HAWK SAM battery. The HAWK crew insisted they had detected, and tracked, an Iraqi MiG-25, and blamed a USAF E-3A AWACS for jamming them, and planting false IFF information in their system. This would not be the last time that the Iranians would blame the Americans for interfering with their radars and communications, nor was it the only IRIAF F-14 to be shot down by Iranian air defences.

POP!

In late 1981 Iranian Tomcats started encountering new opponents – mainly Mirage F 1EQs and MiG-25s. The first confirmed Mirage F 1EQ kill was recorded on 3 December 1981, this aircraft being one of six operating against Iranian positions on the southern sector of the front. The victory came in a two-week period of intensive air-to-air battles when IRIAF F-14s claimed a total of 16 Iraqi fighters, including six Mirages.

Although remaining operational in large numbers, and extremely dangerous for any Iraqi pilot they encountered, Iran's F-14s fleet was suffering from continued engine maladies. These were similar to the problems encountered by the US Navy, which lost up to 80 F-14s in different engine-related accidents. Although the Iranian Tomcat pilots do not readily admit it, the TF30 powerplant caused problems for even the most experienced aviators, as Capt Nuzran recalled:

'Two F-14s were standing their weekly night alert duty at Khatami. For the most part, this mission was extremely boring, as we had never yet experienced a night-time alert in the war with Iraq – IrAF pilots were no night fliers. However, Russian and East German "instructors" were about to change this. Just after midnight on 22 March 1982, our GCI detected a lone Iraqi "fast-mover" crossing our border, and the alert was sounded. An IrAF MiG-25RB was intending to take photographs of our bases and air defences, probably starting with Yawhi air base The radar tracked it at Mach 2 and plotted its course towards Mehrabad. We had little doubt that the aeroplane was flown by an experienced Russian or East German pilot, but this would not deter us from trying to shoot him down.

Mirage F 1EQ 4010 was part of the first batch of 16 Dassault fighters delivered to Iraq in 1981. After a lengthy introduction into service, the type suffered heavy losses to IRIAF Tomcats during several engagements over the northern Persian Gulf in December 1981. Both small and fast, the F 1EQ had good endurance and could employ effective weapons. However, better-trained and combat-experienced Iranian pilots, as well as the Mirage's poor RWR, which made it vulnerable to the AIM 54, eventually neutralised any advantages the F 1 might have had. Iranian pilots had more respect for the R 550-armed MiG-21 and the high-flying MiG-25 (*Dassault via authors*)

'From the time the alert was sounded, the crews had five to six minutes to make their final checks and get their Tomcats out of the hardened aircraft shelter. Their jets were armed in "two each" configuration – two AIM-54s, two AIM-7s and two AIM-9s. The Tomcat handles well on the ground and moves very easily – learning to steer it very precisely is no problem. After moving to the runway, both pilots lit their afterburners, setting them to 100 per cent power before starting their take-off runs. As they began to move, a loud "pop" was heard by the lead Tomcat's RIO, as well as all of us on the ground. The left engine of his F-14 had stalled, causing asymmetric thrust during the take-off run – a very bad thing.

'The pilot screamed over the radio to his wingman, who was just behind him, to "Abort! Abort!" Hearing this, the wingman shut down both of his engines and applied the brakes as hard as was safely possible. His nose-wheel gear leg was compressed very hard towards the surface, almost causing the Tomcat to go nose-down into the runway with its tail up. If your aeroplane flips over onto its back you cannot eject – you'll be crushed. At best you'll eject directly into the ground and be killed.

'After warning his wingman, the leader concentrated on his own situation as his Tomcat began to veer off the runway at high speed. Unable to stop, he ordered his RIO to prepare to eject when he saw a ground control approach (GCA) structure looming ahead of the runaway F-14. He then ejected both of them. Just a few seconds after the engine had stalled, the crew was floating towards the earth some 50 metres from where their F-14 had stopped after its impact with the GCA equipment. Nobody was hurt, and the Tomcat didn't catch fire after the crash, allowing it be repaired and flown once again nine years later.'

Maj Ali explained the engine problems that blighted the F-14, and the IRIAF's solution to them:

'Although our Tomcats operated from ground bases only, all take-offs were conducted at full afterburner. Stalls associated with afterburner "pop" were not that common, and take-offs with afterburner couldn't, and didn't, compound the TF30-PW-414's already bad stall characteristics. The pops or bangs often heard during these take-off stalls were caused by fuel that had accumulated inside the afterburner due to delayed ignition. The afterburner exhaust nozzles on the TF30 engines

During the war's early stages, many aircraft were taken from storage and sent into battle still wearing IIAF titles, like this F-14A at TFB 7. Additional Tomcats were returned to service in 1981 as the organisation of the IRIAF slowly recovered and more pilots and technicians were released from prison after having been 'rehabilitated'. At the same time, several clandestine shipments of spare parts and equipment reportedly arrived from the USA. By the end of the year the IRIAF had 60 operational F-14As (*authors' collection*)

are fully closed until the afterburner ignites. Any delay in ignition could result in this pooled fuel causing a back pressure or high pressure spike to go back through the TF30 fan ducts. This could cause the engine compressor fan, and the whole engine, to stall.

'It was 1983 before we learned from the Americans – who were permanently monitoring our operations, and knew about almost every one of our problems – that by pre-positioning the afterburner exhaust nozzle to a slightly open position in anticipation of afterburner ignitions, we could prevent most of the "pop stalls".'

OPENING THE SEASON

Constantly improving maintenance despite intensive flying and almost permanent combat, the Iranians slowly enhanced their F-14s' capabilities so that in 1982 they were successful against Iraqi MiG-25s. The first 'Foxbats' had arrived in Iraq in early 1980, but they were initially under strict Soviet control. The USSR had originally deployed ten MiG-25PD (export) – equipped with Smerch A-1 radar and R-60 short-range missiles – and MiG-25RBs to Shoaibah air base, south of Basra, together with a regiment of 16 MiG-21MFs and 20 MiG-23s to guard them.

By August 1980, a total of 24 MiG-25s were in Iraq. They were mainly used for training, which was then interrupted by the outbreak of war. But the IRIAF bombed Shoaibah so heavily and inflicted such grievous losses on Soviet and East German-flown MiG-21s and MiG-23s that they were forced to evacuate to the remote H-3 air base in western Iraq.

Although by early 1981 four MiG-25s had been placed under Iraqi control, the IrAF had suffered such losses that qualified pilots became scarce. Consequently, the type's full service integration was postponed, and all operational missions undertaken by 'Iraqi' 'Foxbats' during that year were flown by Soviet and East German pilots. By April 1981 only four additional MiG-25RBs had been assigned to A Flight, 1st Fighter-Reconnaissance Squadron, IrAF, which also flew few Hunter FR Mk 10s and MiG-21RFs. Later it was to receive four MiG-25PDs under Soviet control. Officially, they were operated by the same unit's B Flight.

The first known engagement between IrAF MiG-25s and IRIAF F-14s came after a period of intensive air-to-air fighting involving F-4s and F-5s from Vahdati air base, near Dezful, and IrAF MiG-21s and MiG-23s from several airfields between Salman Pak and Basra. At first, the Iraqis suffered heavily in these battles in late April and early May 1981. But then they rushed in two MiG-21MF squadrons whose jets were armed with French-supplied Matra R 550 Magic Mk I air-to-air missiles. Both units were also staffed by pilots specially trained in aerial combat. They were to inflict telling losses on the IRIAF.

Indeed, the situation became so precarious that the Iranians were compelled to deploy a full unit of Tomcats to Vahdati to re-establish air superiority in the area. Moving a squadron of F-14s so close to the frontline was a risky business, as Vahdati was the target of frequent Iraqi air and artillery attacks. There was, though, no other choice. Maj Ali recalled:

'Ten 82nd TFS Tomcats (two others had to return to Esfahan due to engine-related problems) arrived at TFB 4 on 15 May 1981. Only two hours after their arrival, four F-14s and two F-4Es established a CAP west of the airfield. Within minutes they detected six MiG-23BNs covered by four MiG-21s. We attacked and two MiG-21s were shot down, both by Sidewinders – one by F-14A 3-6020 and the second by one of the accompanying Phantom IIs.

'A few minutes later the lead F-14A RIO detected a MiG-25RB closing at high speed, but still inside Iraqi airspace. The pilot immediately turned to attack, and within seconds a single AIM-54A was launched at the target, which was then still 108 km (67 miles) away. The excellent "Siren" RWR of the MiG-25RB detected the threat in time, however. Although the PSTT emission – needed to supply the AIM-54 with final targeting data for engagements at such long ranges – from the AWG-9 lasted less than two seconds, the Soviet pilot was warned.

'He immediately turned as tightly as possible away from the border and thundered west at 2800 kmh (1750 mph), activating his ECM as he went. The combination of this powerful manoeuvre and the ECM gave mixed results. The "Foxbat" moved towards the edge of the Phoenix envelope, but the missile had a built-in home-on-jam capability and the weapon passed close by its target nevertheless, exploding behind the jet. That MiG pilot was lucky. Most of the shrapnel missed, but his aeroplane was still damaged and he had to make an emergency landing at Shoaibah.'

The F-14 and MiG-25 were to fight several spectacular engagements later in the war, but the first known battle between the two had ended in a draw. The strategic situation, however, changed considerably. The Iraqis cancelled their offensive on Vahdati, and several days later the 82nd TFS pulled back to TFB 8, its job done. TFB 4 F-4 pilot Maj Daryush recalled the impact of this encounter:

'TFB 4 was like a "Wild West" fort surrounded by hostile Indians, so the F-14s appeared there like the cavalry coming to the rescue to drive the Indians away! Before the Tomcats showed up, our morale as a fighting force was low, and decreasing. To lose so many pilots and aeroplanes in such a short period without any result was unknown to our unit. Until then the Iraqis ran from our fighters more often than not, and many of our pilots saw this as cowardice. When they didn't run we shot

From the autumn of 1981, the Iraqis started using MiG-25RBs to bomb the Khark oil installations. Initially, careful timing enabled the Iraqis to avoid patrolling Iranian F-14s, but in September and December 1982 two MiG-25RBs were shot down. A survivor of the Iran–Iraq War and the Gulf War of 1991, this upgraded, and wingless, MiG-25RBT (serialled 25107) was found by US troops at al-Taqaddum air base in July 2003. The interceptor had been buried to avoid it being spotted from the air by Coalition aircraft (*US DoD*)

them down. That May we learned they weren't cowards, and I now feel strongly that the IrAF's reluctance to engage us was mainly caused by the limited range of their aircraft – they were usually short of fuel.'

Clearly, the Iraqis, Soviets and East Germans did not welcome this development, and their situation was to worsen still further. Indeed, by the autumn of 1981 the IrAF had been so severely weakened by losses that it could barely muster 140 combat-capable aircraft. The Iraqis now had little choice but to increase the use of their MiG-25s. It was the only type superior to Iranian interceptors in at least one aspect – speed. Disbelieving Iraqi reports of the effectiveness of Iranian F-14s, the Soviets and East Germans were keen to see how the 'Foxbats' performed against Iran's US-built systems. Consequently, the training of IrAF crews on MiG-25s was further intensified. Maj Ali commented on the Iraqi 'Foxbat' pilots he encountered in combat:

'They were selected by a stringent screening process. They were judged on their flying skills, experience and mental abilities, and not just their loyalty to the regime. These pilots were smart, and the IrAF's best bar none. Many were trained by the British, Indians and French before being qualified for MiG-25s by the Russians and the Eastern Germans. Even if they were only equal to average IRIAF pilots, they were brave and daring. We were lucky there were fewer than 20 of them at this point in the war.'

After their first encounter with F-14s, the IrAF 'Foxbats' appeared over the frontline again in October 1981. Initially, they flew reconnaissance sorties over Khark, before making their first strikes. These early missions were not particularly encouraging for the IrAF. The Soviets and East Germans needed time to learn how to calibrate the jet's 'Peleng-D' navigational-attack system, while the pilots also had to learn how to fly the aircraft precisely if they were to drop their weapons anywhere near the target. Reacting to the MiG-25RBs' appearance over Khark, the IRIAF intensified F-14 patrols. The situation quietened for several months.

In the spring of 1982, however, the IRIAF tracked at least a dozen MiG-25 flights along the front. Usually, they were operating at altitudes of more than 62,000 ft (19,000 m) and at speeds around Mach 2.2. IRIAF interceptors were often scrambled, but they usually lacked the speed to engage the 'Foxbats'. By then Iraqi MiG-25Ps had also started to penetrate Iranian airspace. Sooner or later, the next encounter with the Tomcats would be inevitable.

'FOXBAT' HUNTERS

MiG-25RBs participated in the first Iraqi air offensive against Khark Island, which was launched in August 1982. Operating at high speeds and altitudes, they proved exceptionally difficult to intercept. For even the best and most aggressive IRIAF Tomcat crews, a successful 'Foxbat' interception was the ultimate exercise in precision flying and high-speed operations, causing heavy cockpit workload. Yet, like all IRIAF pilots, those of the 8th TFW were eager to attempt an engagement.

This eagerness intensified after September 1982, when IrAF MiG-25RBs started flying missions deeper into Iran, striking civilian targets and causing dozens of deaths. Iraqi 'Foxbat' operations grew to such a degree that F-14As deployed at Mehrabad had to conduct 24-hour CAPs over the Iranian capital. During these difficult times, patrols were limited to nocturnal hours or during Friday Prayers. CAPs were initially conducted at 30,000 ft, but when a MiG-25 was detected, the F-14s would climb to 40,000 ft and accelerate to Mach 1+. The 'Foxbats', however, usually operated at between 60,000 and 70,000 ft and flew between Mach 1.9 and 2.4.

They proved evasive targets, and it took the IRIAF some time to learn how to intercept them – mainly by changing patrol altitudes, positions and speeds. F-14A crews would also occasionally act as fighter-controllers, directing other fighters to intercept Iraqi MiG-25s, as well as Tu-22B, Tu-22KD and Tu-16 bombers.

It is not known exactly when the IrAF lost its first 'Foxbat' to IRIAF Tomcats. On 4 May 1982, an IrAF defector explained to his Syrian interrogators that Iraq had lost 98 fighters and 33 pilots to Iranian F-4s and F-14s. This total included a MiG-25 to an F-14-launched Phoenix missile. The Iraqis were not likely to reveal such details without good reason. What is confirmed, however, is that it came when the 'hunting season' for Iraqi MiG-25s was opened by the IRIAF's 8th TFW.

At 1240 hrs on 16 September 1982, two F-14As on a CAP between Bushehr and Khark were advised by GCI of a single contact approaching Khark at 70,000 ft and travelling close to Mach 3. The Tomcats turned into the threat and the leader's RIO activated his AWG-9 to start the interception of what was clearly a MiG-25RB. After few minutes the target was acquired. The AWG-9 established a targeting file and a single AIM-54A was fired from a range of over 100 km (60 miles). There was no reaction from the Iraqi MiG, and the missile swiftly cut the distance to the target and slammed into it, creating a giant ball of fire. The pilot was reported to have ejected over the sea, but he could not be found by Iranian helicopters – the shark-infested waters of the Persian Gulf were never a promising area for search and rescue operations.

According to Iranian sources, this was the first confirmed kill of an Iraqi 'Foxbat' by IRIAF F-14s, although the Iraqi defector had claimed that one had been lost prior to this date. The victory confirmed that the AWG-9 and AIM-54 could engage and destroy MiG-25s flying at almost Mach 3. There would be other successes too, but the IrAF remained defiant. On 22 September a MiG-25RB roared high over Tehran.

Clearly, the IRIAF could not tolerate such Iraqi missions over the Iranian capital. Therefore, F-14As of the 72nd TFS, deployed at Mehrabad, were always well supplied with AIM-54s, as these offered the best chance of intercepting Iraqi aircraft operating in the area. Additionally, three F-14As normally used for testing and training purposes had their AWG-9s and communication equipment modified to allow them to operate as 'mini-AWACS'. These jets not only provided early warning coverage for the Tehran area, but also guidance for other fighters – particularly F-4Es from TFB 1 – intercepting Iraqi bombers. Their patrols frequently lasted 12 hours, during which time they would refuel from a KC 707 up to five times.

Despite the Tehran overflights, the next engagement with 'Foxbats' took place near Khark. On 1 December 1982, an F-14A flown by Maj Shahram Rostami was on a CAP between Khark and Bandar-e-Khomeini, covering a convoy of merchant ships en route to Bandar Abbas. After two hours on station, and shortly after refuelling from a

KC 707, Rostami was alerted by GCI of a single contact approaching from the north at 70,000 ft and Mach 2.3 – a MiG-25. Rostami's F-14A was at 40,000 ft and flying at only Mach 0.4 at the time. GCI control warned him that the bandit was rapidly closing to 113 km (61 miles), so the crew had to work fast.

While Rostami accelerated, his RIO tried to acquire the target, but his efforts were briefly hindered when the MiG pilot activated his own ECM systems and swiftly closed to 71 km (38 miles). Despite the jamming, Rostami's RIO was

able to obtain a positive radar lock-on and fire a single AIM-54A in a snap-up engagement from 64 km (34 miles) as the F-14A accelerated to Mach 1.5 and climbed to 45,000 ft. The missile separated properly, the engine ignited almost instantly and the hefty Phoenix thundered away trailing white smoke. After the launch, Rostami turned his Tomcat slightly to the west and reduced speed and altitude to avoid approaching the MiG too fast. He held the target just inside the radar envelope.

As time passed, and the MiG continued to cut the distance, Rostami turned back to starboard. Just then, the computer-calculated time-to-impact on the weapons panel counters reached zero. The hit symbol illuminated on the radar screen, and moments later ground control confirmed that the Iraqi fighter had disappeared from their radar scope. The MiG-25RB crashed into the sea. The pilot could not be found despite an intensive IrAF SAR operation.

The Iraqi/Soviet 'Foxbat' community vowed to take revenge after this loss, and on 4 December two MiG-25PDs penetrated the airspace over northern Iran and tried to intercept an airliner flying from Turkey as it passed over Tabriz. While searching for a target, the MiGs separated. Unknown to them, the IRIAF had vectored a single 81st TFS F-14A, flown by Maj Toufanian, into the area. His AWG-9 was on standby, and only the 'Combat Tree' equipment was being used in his approach to minimum AIM-54 firing distance. As soon as the radar was activated, the 'Foxbat's' on-board RWR warned the pilot of the F-14's presence and the MiG-25PD immediately accelerated. The Tomcat crew watched in awe as their target attempted to out-turn the AIM-54 that they had fired at it.

This time, the Phoenix malfunctioned. It missed, passing behind the 'Foxbat', but Maj Toufanian, who was one of the first, and most uncompromising, Iranian F-14 pilots, powered his jet up to Mach 2.2 and went off in pursuit. After the first Phoenix had missed, the Iraqi pilot slowed down, obviously feeling safe. But he had effectively signed his own death warrant, for a second AIM-54 blew the 'Foxbat' out of the sky.

IRAQI GENERALS MEET IRANIAN TOMCATS

As well as battling 'Foxbats' over the Persian Gulf in October and November 1982, 81st and 82nd TFS F-14As were also engaged in

During the summer and autumn of 1981, the IrAF intensified its operations against Iranian oil exports from Khark Island. Here, the southern and eastern part of the Khark installations can be seen, including the storage depots and one of the two T-shaped jetties from which the world's largest supertankers could be loaded. For seven years, dozens of fierce aerial battles were fought in the skies over Khark between the F-14s and IrAF fighters. The Tomcat crews enjoyed some of their greatest successes in this area, but also suffered most of their losses here too (*US DoD*)

supporting F-4Es from Nojeh air base. The Phantom IIs were involved in Operation *Muharram*, which was undertaken by the Iranian Army on the front between Eyne-Khosh and Musiyan. During the fighting, the Iranians penetrated Iraqi lines and inflicted severe losses.

The situation became so critical that two high-ranking Iraqi officers – Maj Gen Maher Abdul Rasheed of the Army General Staff and III Corps CO and Lt Gen Abdel Jabar Muhsen, IV Corps assistant CO and Army spokesman – decided to inspect the frontline. The generals feared losses similar to those suffered during the Iranian offensives in the spring of 1982, when the Iraqi Army lost two divisions of troops and their equipment.

On the morning of 20 November 1982, the two generals boarded an armed Mi-8 'Hip' helicopter piloted by Capt S Mousa. They were escorted by two other Mi-8s and a single Mi-25 'Hind' gunship, which also acted as pathfinder. Overhead, this formation was to be escorted by four MiG-21s and four MiG-23s, which were to be replaced by additional fighters as their fuel ran low.

At around 1040 hrs, flying at 40,000 ft and only 8 km (five miles) from the Iraqi border, an IRIAF KC 707 tanker and two F-14s were waiting for a pair of F-4Es to approach for in-flight refuelling, before heading into Iraq. The two Tomcats, led by Capt Khosrodad, flew a race-track pattern, with one continuously scanning the airspace over the border with its AWG-9 radar. Five minutes later, just as the first Phantom IIs started receiving fuel, Khosrodad's AWG-9 acquired several targets closing slowly on the tanker from the west at low level, and already within AIM-54 range.

Recalling the standing order not to fly into Iraqi airspace, or to leave the tanker unprotected, Khosrodad decided to attack, but only after he had ordered his wingman – whose jet was armed with Sparrows and Sidewinders only – to stay with the KC 707 and the two Phantom IIs. Khosrodad then dived towards the west.

He and his RIO fired two AIM-54s in quick succession, followed by two AIM-7E-4s some ten seconds later. They were gratified to notice that two of the targets had apparently disappeared from the radar display. The Iraqis, however, were completely unaware of the F-14s' presence. The first first indication Capt Mousa got that things were going wrong was when the pilot of an escorting Mi-8 flying two kilometres ahead of him shouted a warning that three of the escorting fighters were falling out of the sky in flames! He told Mousa to make a hard turn to the right to evade the debris as it fell to earth all around them.

Seconds later, one of the MiG pilots also shouted a warning. They had no idea what was attacking them, but 'strongly' suggested that the VIP Mi-8 leave the area immediately! As the stricken MiGs plunged earthwards, Mousa found himself in complete agreement with the surviving escorts. The trip to the front by Gens Rasheed and Muhsen was over before it had even started.

Having expended all his Phoenix and Sparrows to down one MiG-21 and two MiG-23s in under a minute, Khosrodad returned to the tanker. He advised the Phantom II crews of the presence of Iraqi fighters in the area, but his AWG-9 had apparently not detected the slow-flying Mi-8s travelling at low level between the hills.

ATTRITION

Several Western publications state that between 16 January and 18 February 1983, IRIAF air defences shot down no fewer than 80 Iraqi aircraft, of which at least 24 were credited to Tomcats. Extensive research within the small Iranian fighter pilot community has proved, however, that 'only a few' kills were scored during this period. Even official Iranian reports describe this phase of the war as 'very quiet'.

Realising that the conflict had developed into a war of attrition, the IRIAF High Command had, accordingly, ordered all units to conduct operations with care. Nevertheless, the Iranians started employing a new strategy in which interceptors and SAM sites were combined to create 'killing fields' for Iraqi fighters. Not much is known about this tactic, probably because it remains valid, but it seems to have included F-4s or F-14s as the 'hammer', either dragging or forcing the Iraqis onto the SAM 'anvil'. On 16 January, for example, three unidentified Iraqi fighters (probably J-6s, which were Chinese MiG-19 copies) are known to have been shot down. They were followed by a Mirage and a MiG-23 on the 21st, a Su-20 on the 27th and another MiG-23 on the 29th.

Despite Iranian caution, fighting continued at a similar pace for the rest of 1983, with both sides flying continuous strikes against various targets. The IrAF, now reinforced by more than 200 new aircraft acquired from China and the USSR, continued to suffer losses. Even the upgraded MiG-25s, fitted with the newest Soviet avionics and ECM systems, continued to prove vulnerable to IRIAF interceptors.

On 6 August, two MiG-25PDs used Turkish airspace to make a sudden appearance near Tabriz. But their plot was foiled by a single F-14A from TFB 1 that was on CAP nearby, its AWG-9 in standby mode to avoid revealing its presence. The Iranian crew finally powered up their radar and fired a Phoenix once the MiGs had flown deep into the AIM-54's engagement envelope. As with previous MiG-25 interceptions of this kind, the Iraqi pilots reacted rapidly once they realised the danger they were in. Both fighters turned round and picked up speed, but the AIM-54 cut the range and detonated near one of them, damaging its engines and fins. The MiG was mortally wounded but still flying. Its pilot tried to nurse it out of Iranian airspace, but lacked support from his wingman, who had made good his escape.

Not far away, below the scene of this drama, IRIAF Capt Kazem Zarif-Khadem was leading a pair of napalm and AIM-9-armed F-5E Tiger IIs in an attack on Iraqi positions. As usual, Zarif-Khadem was flying at very low level, busily

An Iraqi MiG-23BN rolls away at very low level over forward Iranian positions after dropping its bombs. IRIAF F-14s caused exceptionally heavy losses to the type early in the war, much to the disappointment of the IrAF, which throught that the Soviet fighter would be a match for the Tomcat (*authors' collection*)

navigating his way over the rough terrain towards the target. Suddenly, he was amazed to see a MiG-25 crossing his path both low and fast. Zarif-Khadem immediately jettisoned his bombs and drop tank, rammed the throttle to full afterburner and turned in behind the stricken MiG. Seconds later, and in a 'deep-six' position, he fired both his Sidewinders.

The missiles were halfway to the target when the Iraqi pilot noticed the attack and broke. But it was too late, for both AIM-9s hit home and exploded – the pilot ejected and was recovered by the Iraqis. This was the fifth 'Foxbat' claimed by IRIAF interceptors, and its loss caused the IrAF to halt similar forays into Iranian airspace.

TOMCATS SUPREME

On the morning of 26 February 1984, a single F-14A set a trap for a large strike package of IrAF MiG-23BNs. The leading Iraqi fighter was shot down by an AIM-54A, after which the Tomcat engaged in a dogfight and downed two more Iraqi jets using Sidewinders. This clash was a warning of what was to come, with more engagements between one or two Tomcats and much larger Iraqi formations. Capt Javad explained:

'The F-14 had become so feared by the IrAF by then that when they were not airborne over Iran, Iraqi MiGs and Sukhois filled the sky like the "birds of the Howr al-Howeizeh", bombing our positions with ease. If there was no Tomcat over Khark or Tehran, the Iraqis would immediately attempt to strike. And it worked the other way around too – wherever IRIAF F-14s showed up, the Iraqis ran away.'

This was probably why Iranian supreme commander Akbar H Rafsanjani specifically boasted about the type's effectiveness in a speech he gave on 26 April 1984:

'Our air force is now more potent than in the first days of the war. We have suffered no F-14 losses so far, and the F-14 is the kind of aircraft the enemy does not even dare to get close to.'

The days when the Iranian regime had doubts about the worth of its Tomcat fleet were obviously over. Attempting to disprove such statements by exposing the weakness of Iran's air defences, IrAF High Command issued a formal warning of the implementation of an exclusion zone around Khark Island. The Iraqis also announced a blockade of shipping to this vital oil terminal, but they lacked the ability to enforce it. But the real intention was to make shipping companies reluctant to use the Khark terminal.

The IrAF backed up these threats by making greater use of Super Frelon helicopters and Super Etendard fighter bombers armed with AM 39 Exocet anti-ship missiles for strikes on shipping along the Iranian coast. While the actual mission effectiveness of both

Defending Khark Island and other local oil installations, and ensuring their continued use for exporting oil, was vital to the Iranian war effort. Therefore, all available resources were invested in the defence of the area. From 1981 onwards, the 81st and 82nd TFS flew near constant CAPs over this region, and by 1986 the two units had set up a semi-permanent detachment of F-14s at TFB 6 Bushehr. Most of aerial victories scored by the IRIAF's Tomcat force were claimed in the area shown in this map (*authors' collection*)

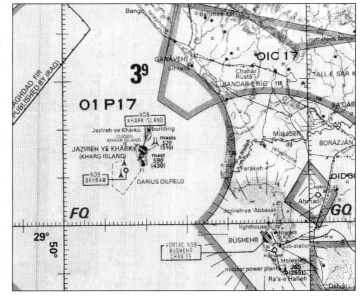

For eight long years the Iraqis made a determined effort to disable the Khark Island oil storage and loading complex, using surface-to-surface missiles, Kh-22/AS-4 and KSR-5/AS-6 air-to-ground missiles and fighter-bombers dropping unguided bombs or firing guided bombs and missiles from stand-off ranges. MiG-25s and Tu-22s also performed a number of bombing missions, with variable success. IRIAF Tomcats frustrated most IrAF attempts to knock out Khark, allowing the oil to continue to flow to waiting supertankers. But never before had so many air strikes been directed at a single target for so long (*authors' collection*)

platforms was far from perfect, the Iraqis – and, to some extent, the international press – boasted about the Exocet, and greatly over-claimed its successes.

On 1 March 1984, for example, the IrAF stated that it had hit six ships in the Persian Gulf with Exocets. Yet, at 0913 hrs that very morning, 82nd TFS F-14s had shot down an IrAF Su-22M during a short combat near the Iraqi al-Bakr and al-Omayeh offshore platforms, south of the Al Faw Peninsula. No Iraqi fighters came anywhere near ships sailing between Bandar-e-Khomeini and Bushehr, nor, of course, the Iranian Tomcats. The Iraqis attempted another raid on 24 March, sending at least four aircraft to bomb Khark.

The threat now posed by IRIAF F-14As was illustrated not only by the IrAF's reluctance to engage them in combat, but also by the actions of the Royal Saudi Air Force (RSAF). The Saudis did not believe Iraqi reports of the massive destruction wrought on Iranian coastal shipping by Exocet attacks, or the heavy casualties suffered by the IRIAF in aerial combat. Proof that the Iranians were still a force to be reckoned with in the region came on 25 March when Tomcats downed an IrAF Tu-22B bomber over the Majnoon islet, in the Howeizeh marshes. When two more Tu-22Bs were destroyed with AIM-54As on 6 April over the Persian Gulf, the RSAF ordered its fighters to stay away from areas in which IRIAF Tomcats were known to operate.

The F-14 units were certainly active during this period, and according to TFB 8 pilot Capt Abolfazl Mehreganfar, between mid 1983 and mid 1984 Iranian Tomcats flew more sorties than they had ever done. All the maintenance, flying and training paid off, for on 26 July 1984 an F-14 crew claimed the type's first Super Etendard kill (scored with an AIM-54A), although the Iraqi pilot somehow managed to nurse his crippled jet home and crash-land. The IrAF stayed silent about the loss, but halted anti-shipping operations for almost two weeks.

The Super Etendards returned on 7 August, and were again detected – one was downed by a lone F-14A minutes after it had launched two Exocets. The Tomcat crew immediately tried to engage them with its remaining Phoenix round, but it is not known whether they were successful. Although the number of Super Etendards claimed shot down by IRIAF interceptors in 1984 had now risen to three (the first fell to an F-4 on 2 April), the French later declared that four of the five fighter-bombers leased to Iraq were returned in 1985. Even today there is no firm confirmation of either version of events.

The five Super Etendards supplied to Iraq were obtained by diverting aircraft ordered by the French Navy. Under a loan agreement, Dassault-Breguet was to pay the Navy FFr 140 million for each jet at the end of the loan period. It also committed itself to build replacement aircraft should

Iraqi losses exceed two, even though the production line would by then be closed. It is unclear whether Dassault honoured these commitments.

On 11 August 1984, in what was seen as a reaction to the losses, Baghdad radio claimed three Iranian Tomcats 'shot down into the sea off Bushehr during an air combat'. Aside from the fact that IRIAF F-14s never operated in formations larger than a pair, closer examination of this claim proved it to have been based on Iranian reports of a single Tomcat loss in this area on the same day. For years, IRIAF records were based on the assumption that the crew, Col Mohammad-Hashem All-e-Agha and Maj Abolfazl Zerafati, had defected to Saudi Arabia.

Other sources, probably influenced by Iraqi claims, claimed that the Tomcat had been shot down by a Super 530F-1 missile fired by an Iraqi Mirage F 1EQ interceptor. Careful investigation, however, has proved that no Iraqi aircraft were anywhere near the Tomcat, that All-e-Agha's AWG-9 was functioning normally and that contact with him was lost during his return to Bushehr from some kind of 'special mission'.

Years after the war, during an oil exploration mission off Khark, the missing Tomcat was found in the water with the remains of the crew still strapped in the cockpit. Official records later suggested that All-e-Agha's Tomcat had been shot down by an 'enemy SAM while escorting cargo ships in the Persian Gulf', yet few Iraqi SAMs boasted such range.

As far as can be ascertained, All-e-Agha and Zerafati were victims of a 'friendly' MIM-23 whose crew mistook their Tomcat for an Iraqi bomber. This was the third F-14A to be lost during the war, and each of them had been caused by the over zealous Khark SAM site. Yet another Tomcat fell to this battery on 24 March 1985, when Capt Seyed-Hossein Hosseini and 1Lt Ali Eqbali-Moqadam were shot down.

Despite Iranian records indicating that all the Tomcats lost in the early years of the war were 'own goals', a US Department of Defense file states that in 1983 the Iraqis supplied the wreckage of several Iranian aircraft to the Soviets, including part of an F-14A and a badly damaged AIM-54A that was found near the same wreck. The circumstances under which this Tomcat was lost remain unknown, but this information was confirmed by Vafiq al-Samerai, the former head of Iraqi Military Intelligence. He stated that the remains of an Iranian F-14 had been loaded into a Soviet transport aircraft at al-Taqaddum air base, west of Baghdad.

There were, of course, several cases of F-14As suffering combat damage. Apart from the one hit by MiG-21 debris in October 1980 and another damaged in a dogfight with two MiG-23s in April 1981, a third example was safely brought down by its pilot in 1982. The jet's belly was riddled with bullets, one of which had penetrated the fuselage near the cockpit. The circumstances surrounding this action remain unknown.

ENDLESS BATTLES OVER THE GULF

For most of 1985 the defence of Khark, and visiting oil tankers, remained the top priority for the IRIAF's F-14s. The Iraqis opened the New Year by hitting a number of ships. Tomcats of the 8th TFW brought an end to these operations on 14 January when they shot down their first Mirage F 1EQ-5 – this version was fitted with Agave radar and was compatible with the AM 39 Exocet anti-ship missile. The F-14 crews also accounted for the Exocet that the Iraqi jet had just fired (*text continues on page 62*).

On 11 August 1984, an F-14A flown by Col Mohamad-Hashem All-e-Agha and Maj Abolfazl Zerafati was shot down over the Gulf while escorting Iranian merchant shipping – both crewmen were killed. All-e-Agha was one of the first IIAF pilots to convert onto the Tomcat in the United States, and subsequently served for many years as an instructor on the type in Iran. Following the outbreak of war with Iraq, he flew both combat missions and training sorties with future F-14 crews. All-e-Agha was Deputy CO of TFB 8 and the IRIAF's deputy commander for combat operations at the time of his death (*authors' collection*)

COLOUR PLATES

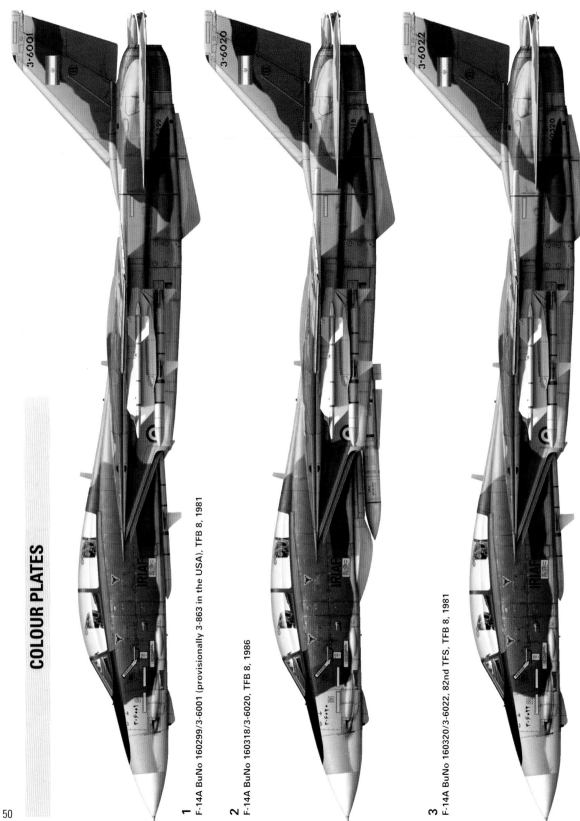

1
F-14A BuNo 160299/3-6001 (provisionally 3-863 in the USA), TFB 8, 1981

2
F-14A BuNo 160318/3-6020, TFB 8, 1986

3
F-14A BuNo 160320/3-6022, 82nd TFS, TFB 8, 1981

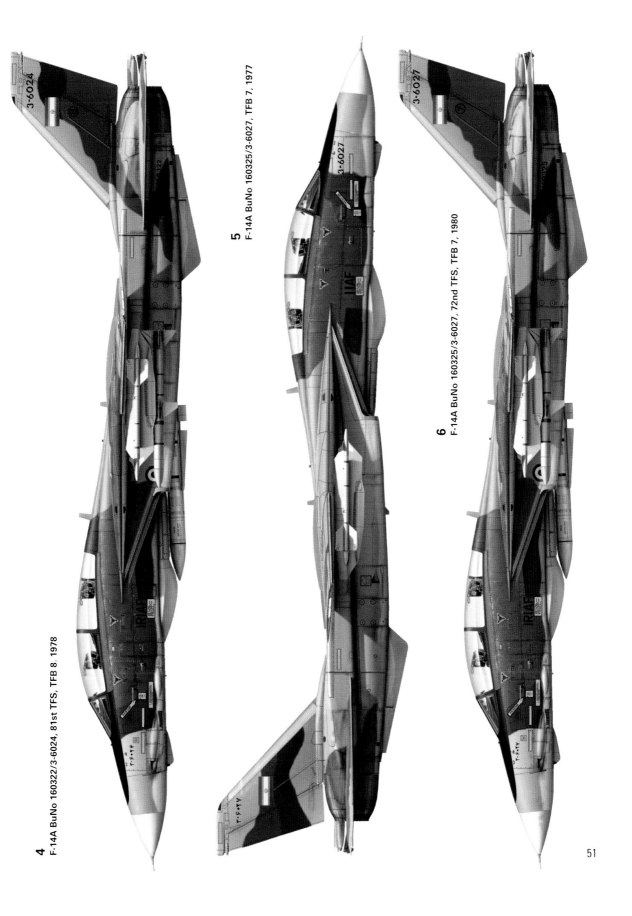

4
F-14A BuNo 160322/3-6024, 81st TFS, TFB 8, 1978

5
F-14A BuNo 160325/3-6027, TFB 7, 1977

6
F-14A BuNo 160325/3-6027, 72nd TFS, TFB 7, 1980

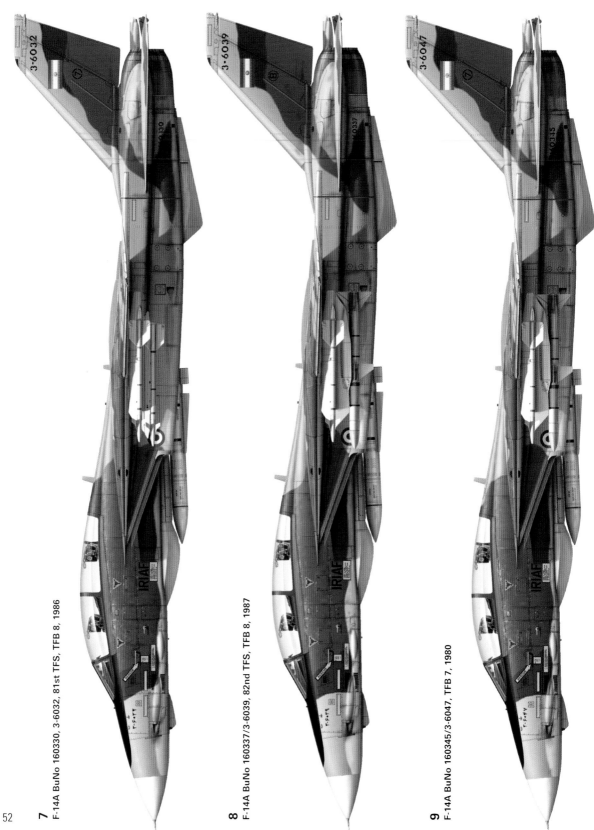

7
F-14A BuNo 160330, 3-6032, 81st TFS, TFB 8, 1986

8
F-14A BuNo 160337/3-6039, 82nd TFS, TFB 8, 1987

9
F-14A BuNo 160345/3-6047, TFB 7, 1980

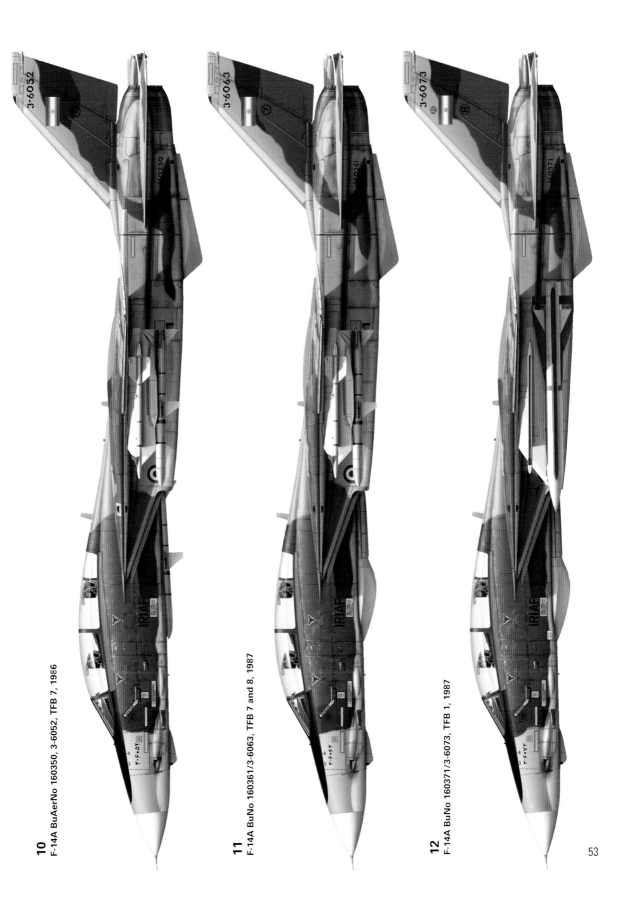

10
F-14A BuAerNo 160350, 3-6052, TFB 7, 1986

11
F-14A BuNo 160361/3-6063, TFB 7 and 8, 1987

12
F-14A BuNo 160371/3-6073, TFB 1, 1987

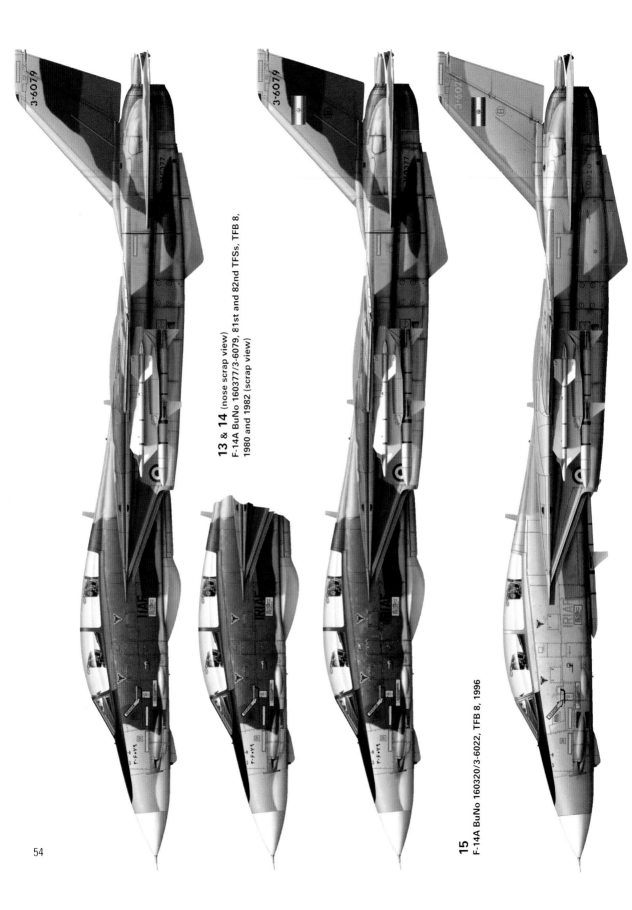

13 & 14 (nose scrap view)
F-14A BuNo 160377/3-6079, 81st and 82nd TFSs, TFB 8,
1980 and 1982 (scrap view)

15
F-14A BuNo 160320/3-6022, TFB 8, 1996

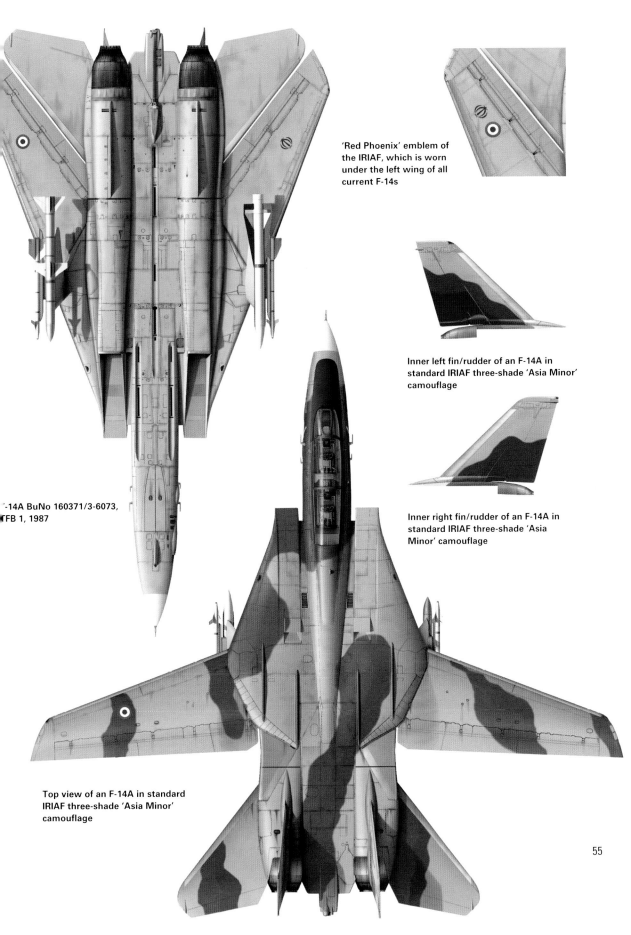

'Red Phoenix' emblem of the IRIAF, which is worn under the left wing of all current F-14s

Inner left fin/rudder of an F-14A in standard IRIAF three-shade 'Asia Minor' camouflage

Inner right fin/rudder of an F-14A in standard IRIAF three-shade 'Asia Minor' camouflage

-14A BuNo 160371/3-6073, FB 1, 1987

Top view of an F-14A in standard IRIAF three-shade 'Asia Minor' camouflage

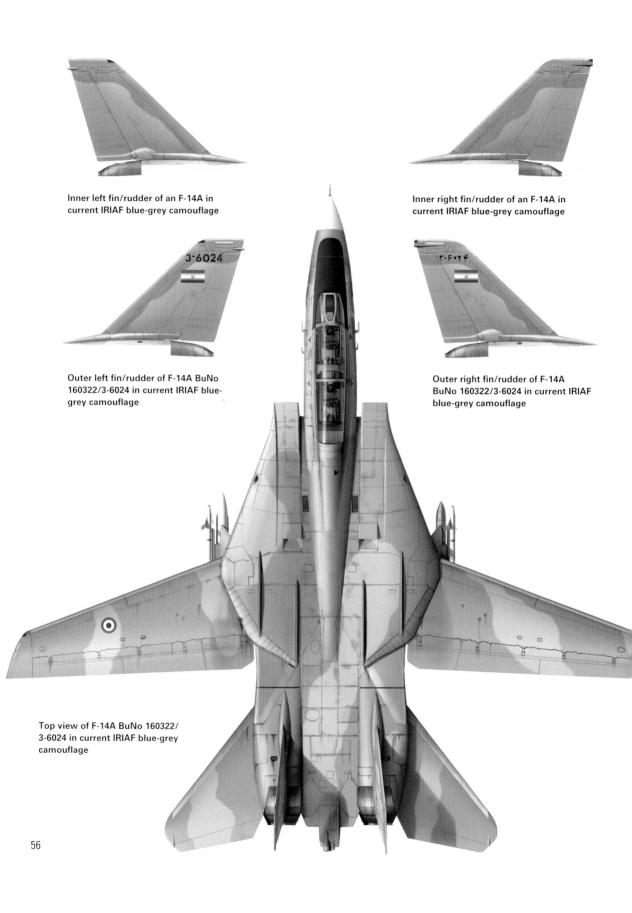

Inner left fin/rudder of an F-14A in current IRIAF blue-grey camouflage

Inner right fin/rudder of an F-14A in current IRIAF blue-grey camouflage

Outer left fin/rudder of F-14A BuNo 160322/3-6024 in current IRIAF blue-grey camouflage

Outer right fin/rudder of F-14A BuNo 160322/3-6024 in current IRIAF blue-grey camouflage

Top view of F-14A BuNo 160322/ 3-6024 in current IRIAF blue-grey camouflage

1

2

3

57

4

5

6

7

8

9

10

11

12

13

14

15

16

17

18

The IrAF introduced the Mirage F 1EQ-5 into service in early 1985. Besides being compatible with the Super 530F-1 air-to-air missiles, this version was equipped with the Cyrano IVM radar, which boasted an air-to-surface mode that enabled it to supply targeting data to the AM 39 Exocet anti-ship missile. After the solution of initial compatibility problems between the aircraft and the missile, the F 1EQ-5 saw widespread service in the 'tanker war' of 1986–87. But operating at a heavy all-up weight at the limit of its endurance over the Persian Gulf saw the Mirage suffer badly at the hands of Iranian F-14s (*authors' collection*)

While most media sources wrote off the IRIAF's Tomcat fleet, and expressed doubts that any aircraft remained combat-capable, the Iranians worked feverishly to keep as many jets as possible operational. By mid 1985 the F-14s had flown over 50,000 hours in combat, yet for every single flight hour some 400 hours of maintenance work was required! IRIAF F-14s usually operated out of the public gaze, conducting CAPs over the Persian Gulf or the plains west of Tehran. This rare fly-past took place on 25 February 1985 (*authors' collection*)

On 26 March, 82nd TFS Tomcats turned the first large Iraqi strike in the northern Persian Gulf for a number of weeks into a catastrophe by downing three Mirages in just two minutes. The IrAF did not return for three weeks, claiming that it was awaiting 'the next shipment of Exocets to arrive from France'. Yet even after these missiles had arrived, the IrAF flew only one anti-shipping mission during the whole of April.

By mid 1985, Iraqi, Soviet and East German MiG-25 pilots had seemingly worked out how best to deal with the Tomcat threat, as not a single 'Foxbat' had been downed since August 1983. They now typically escaped when the F-14s appeared, or managed to hit their targets undisturbed. However, on 20 August 1985 one of four MiG-25RBs heading for Khark was shot down. This would be the last aerial success for the Tomcat in 1985.

The F-14 fleet was now beginning to suffer from a chronic shortage of spare parts, as Maj Ali and Capt Javad recalled:

'By September 1985 we had only 30 to 32 F-14s in combat-capable condition, and only half of these had working AWG-9s at any one time. Our AIM-54 stocks were also depleted. Despite international media claims, Iran received no new Phoenix missiles after October 1978, when the last regular batch of 24 rounds was shipped to the IIAF. A further 24 rounds were awaiting shipment in America when the revolution took place, and these were stopped by the US administration. Eleven more AIM-54s were in final assembly at Hughes, and they became redundant – the US Navy had no use for them. We certainly hadn't received additional AIM-54s, because we would have recognised the "US Navy standard" rounds. Besides, if such a supply had been sanctioned by the US government – which was the case with many clandestine deliveries that arrived in Iran before 1983 – the US Navy would have had to downgrade its own rounds before delivering them.

'On the contrary, by 1986 many of our remaining AIM-54s had passed their shelf life, while a number of others were nearing their

end too. Theoretically, if properly kept and sealed in their containers, the AIM-54s would only have to be checked every three years. After each such period the technicians would check and upgrade their components as required. Such inspections, however, were not carried out during the war with Iraq for many reasons, the most important of which was the shortage of qualified technicians and the lack of spare parts. It was not until 1991 that the IRIAF inspected all remaining AIM-54s and serviced them with spare parts that were now available.

'Six years earlier, the "Irangate" affair of 1985 gave us the opportunity to address our maintenance problems. We requested no less than 1000 spare parts items for our Phoenix missiles, including stocks of batteries, fuses and 200 "service-life extension kits", designated Phase 1M54ALE – this was more than we actually needed, considering the number of rounds remaining in stock at the time. The 1M54ALE kits would return our AIM-54s to life, upgrading them considerably. However, of the 200 requested, only 40 were supplied in a shipment that arrived from Israel on 8 or 9 July 1986.

'The Americans said they could not provide more "without adversely affecting US Navy missile stocks". This made us smile, for we were sure that the Americans never planned to give us more kits anyway. Well, of course, we put everything to good use, and many AIM-54s were returned to full service. I guess that this in turn caused rumours to spread about "additional" Phoenix missiles being delivered to Iran.'

Although never short of opportunities during the war, the IRIAF never tested the F-14's ability to engage six targets simultaneously. As Maj Nuzran explained:

'I never saw an IRIAF Tomcat armed with six AIM-54s. Actually, four Phoenix rounds were seldom carried (except during VIP aeroplane escort missions) due to low missile availability and the weight of such a load. We always had to expect a dogfight, and usually it only took one Iraqi to be shot down to turn the whole formation around and send it back home. The normal load comprised two AIM-54s, two or three AIM-7s and two AIM-9s for the leader of the pair, and six AIM-7s and two AIM-9s for the wingman. On a number of missions – especially during 1984-85 – my Tomcat carried only one AIM-54, and usually I had none at all. Between 1980 and 1988 I fired a total of four AIM-54s in combat. This was more than most other pilots. Three scored direct hits and one missed.'

NON-EXISTENT OPPONENTS AND 'INSANE' PILOTS

IRIAF F-14s were also active in support of Operation *Valfajr-8*, initiated in February 1986. This saw Iranian troops occupy a large part of the Al Faw Peninsula, including the city of Al Faw itself. The IrAF reacted strongly, but suffered big losses to the well-organised IRIAF HAWK SAM batteries. When flying over the front proved too dangerous, the IrAF switched to attacking Iranian cities along the border – Tehran, Esfahan, Arak and the religious city of Qom were also targeted.

Early on 15 February, the Tomcats shot down a MiG-25RB over Arak, again using AIM-54s. Three days later, a Mirage F 1EQ-5 fell to a Phoenix fired by a 72nd TFS F-14A over the Persian Gulf. Another Phoenix fired at a second Mirage missed. The pilot of the downed Iraqi

From early 1983 the IRIAF started combining F-14s with MIM-23A HAWK and MIM-23B I-HAWK SAM batteries to create 'killing-fields' which claimed many young and inexperienced IrAF pilots who had been advised to avoid engagements with Tomcats at any price. Here, an IRIAF MIM-23B I-HAWK SAM site near Dezful can be seen in action in May 1983 firing at Iraqi Su-22s (*authors' collection*)

fighter, Capt Fuad Tait, ejected safely and was taken prisoner.

Ever since the 1979 revolution, and throughout the war with Iraq, there was no end to the distractions suffered by F-14 crews. Not only had many been jailed, tortured and sentenced to death, only to be reprieved by the Iraqi invasion, they now came under observation by officers considered loyal to the regime. They were also watched by so-called 'morale officers'.

Mistrusted by the regime despite their knowledge, experience and achievements, these pilots fought so hard that many aged rapidly. They were ignored by the public and some even had to endure the indignity of being declared 'insane' by their superior officers. An example of the latter occured on 14 March 1986 when an F-14A crew returned from an engagement with a large Iraqi strike force.

Exhausted after a fight with numerous MiG-23s and Su-22s, the pilot mentioned engaging and shooting down a delta-winged 'Mirage 2000' with no national markings, but with large parts of the wings, fuselage and fin painted bright red. That day the crew of an I-HAWK SAM site, forward-deployed in the Ahwaz area, claimed that their radar had been jammed for short periods of time. Both reports were forwarded to IRIAF High Command, which rejected them. It maintained that no Mirage 2000s had been fighting on the Iraqi side, and ignored the fact that a powerful jammer had just been introduced by the Iraqis.

Four more reports from Iranian pilots detailing encounters with 'Mirage 2000s' or 'delta-winged' fighters followed over the coming

On 15 February 1986, this MiG-25RB was shot down by an AIM-54A fired from an F-14A soon after the 'Foxbat' had bombed the city of Arak. The Iraqi pilot ejected safely, but outraged citizens showed no mercy. When news of his death reached the IrAF's 1st FRS, its pilots swore revenge, and several months later Arak was again heavily hit by MiG-25RBs and some 70 civilians killed (*authors' collection*)

This Egyptian Air Force Mirage 5SDE was amongst a handful of jets deployed to Iraq in March 1986 to support the IrAF in the war against Iran. Note that the aircraft's national markings and serial have been sprayed out, but that parts of its fin and spine are still painted in the EAF's distinctive black and orange. The jet also carries a Selenia ALQ-234 ECM pod on its centreline pylon. The Mirage 5SDE's ECM jamming capabilities adversely affected units equipped with F-4s and MIM-23 SAMs, but the F-14 crews encountered no such problems (*authors' collection*)

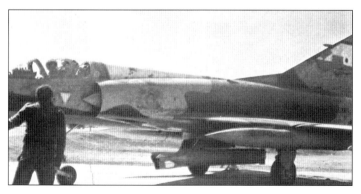

days, and each time the F-4Es engaged these new opponents their radars were jammed. But F-14 radars remained unaffected even if they were flying alongside the Phantom IIs. IRIAF HQ stubbornly refused to accept such reports, and refused to confirm another kill of such a Mirage claimed by an F-4E crew. Indeed, the pilots were accused of 'insanity'! It was simply not accepted that they were fighting a new opponent equipped with unfamiliar ECM systems.

In fact, some Iranian pilots who encountered delta-winged Mirages in combat over the Shatt-al-Arab in March 1986 came to believe that they were the victims of delusions brought about by stress! But in the late 1990s they were shown pictures of Egyptian Air Force Mirage 5SDEs. They had been deployed to Iraq for six weeks at a time with all national markings painted over, and they carried powerful Selenia ALQ-234 ECM pods on their centreline pylons.

PHANTOM II BAIT

Shortly after midnight on 12 July 1986, a combined task force of Iranian warships and Special Boat Service commandos made an unsuccessful attempt to attack the Iraqi al-Omayeh platform in the northern Persian Gulf. Their withdrawal was covered by several IRIAF fighters, which had to beat back a number of Iraqi 'Osa II' missile boats.

During the course of the engagement, an IrAF SA 321 Super Frelon helicopter armed with AM 39 Exocet missiles was spotted landing on the al-Omayeh platform to refuel, obviously in preparation for a strike against Iranian vessels. Although two F-14As were in the air, led by Maj Reza, they could do nothing unless the helicopter was airborne. TFB 6 at Bushehr immediately scrambled an F-4E armed with AGM-65A Maverick air-to-ground missiles.

Closing on al-Omayeh, the Phantom II crew used the ASX-1 TISEO camera to identify their target on the platform's helipad with its engines running. The Iraqis detected the inbound threat and ordered the pilot to stay where he was. The situation was now about to escalate, for as the F-4 came within Maverick range, its pilot was warned by Reza that Iraqi interceptors were closing from the north. The pilot had to work fast. Quickly establishing a lock-on, he fired a Maverick and immediately turned away. The missile scored a direct hit on the Super Frelon, causing a tremendous explosion. Now it was the turn of the Phantom II crew to run. Closing from the south, Reza asked the F-4E pilot to stay in the area and climb, thus enticing the enemy closer. Doing as he was advised, the F-4 pilot followed his instructions:

'Iraqi aircraft is now 25 miles behind you. Now turn left. He's within 20 miles, 15 miles, 10 miles. I have him positively on my radar. Target is locked on. Standby for a kill!'

The Tomcat appeared in the distance and a large plume of smoke erupted beneath it as a Sparrow was despatched. Following the trail, the Phantom II crew suddenly noticed

Despite experiencing growing problems with the reliability of its Tomcat force, the IRIAF was forced to start training new personnel to fly the jet in 1986 due to a shortage of qualified crews. Inexperienced pilots and RIOs had to learn to operate the complex fighter, and all its systems, literally 'on the job' in the heat of combat with numerically-superior Iraqi formations. F-14A 3-6024 is seen here cruising above the clouds during a training mission near Khatami air base in the mid 1980s (*authors' collection*)

the Iraqi MiG-23's silhouette only a few kilometres behind them. Then, a big fireball erupted when the missile hit home and the burning wreckage crashed into the Persian Gulf. The other Iraqi interceptors immediately disengaged.

Once again a MiG-23 had fallen to a well-flown Tomcat. Maj Ali also encountered a number of 'Floggers' during the war, and he recalled:

'The MiG-23 was nowhere near an equal opponent for us. It had good acceleration, which made it easy for the Iraqis to escape, but still they suffered constant losses. From September 1982, the Soviets rushed a large number of R-23R/T medium-range air-to-air missiles to Iraq after Baghdad urgently requested something to counter our AIM-7s. The R-23, however, suffered from problems similar to those that afflicted the AIM-7 during the Vietnam War – it just couldn't hold a lock-on, and certainly couldn't manoeuvre. The IrAF virtually ceased using them after 1984, even if the Iraqis claimed no less than 40 kills with them. In reality, they fired 40 R-23s in combat and scored just two kills – an F-4E and a C-130.'

August 1986 saw the F-14s claim at least five kills, although this run of success came to an abrupt end when, on 3 September, Iraqi news agencies reported that 'three Iranian Phantom IIs' had been flown to Iraq by defecting Iranian pilots. What had happened? In fact, between 24 August and 3 September a total of four IRIAF pilots had flown their aircraft to Iraq – one of these was an F-14. However, the secrets of the aircraft were not revealed either to the Iraqis or the Soviets. Maj Reza explained:

'During the summer of 1986 the CIA and the Pentagon's FTD (Foreign Technologies Division), then operating under the auspices of the USAF's Support Command, and responsible for acquisition and testing of foreign military equipment, mostly aircraft, organised the defection of four IRIAF pilots. The background to this operation – code-named *Night Harvest* – was that the Pentagon was surprised by our ability to maintain and operate US-built aircraft, especially the F-14A. They found four pilots ready to defect – during the war many of us thought about defection at one time or another – including a Tomcat pilot. He flew his aircraft, with two AIM-54s, at low level to Iraq. The RIO was strongly opposed to the defection, and there was a terse conversation in the cockpit once he realised his pilot's intentions.

'The Americans waited for our Tomcat in Iraq. As soon as the aircraft came to stop, it was surrounded by CIA agents. The pilot was taken into US custody and granted asylum in the West, only to be gunned down by unidentified assailants in Switzerland several years later. The RIO was handed over to the Iraqis, who held him as a PoW until 1990.

'As with the Phantom IIs, the Iranian F-14A was given a thorough check. The technicians found they had to repair several systems as the American crew that was to fly the aircraft out of Iraq refused to do so in the state that it had arrived. In fact, one of the Phantom IIs was in such poor condition that it had to be left behind at Tallil air base after the

From 1984 onwards, the Iraqis took delivery of MiG-23MLs that were equipped with R-23 and R-24 air-to-air missiles. These were supplied in response to an IrAF request for a fighter capable of countering Iranian F-4s and F-14s, and their deadly Sparrow and Phoenix missiles. However, as with the MiG-23MS, the more advanced ML proved a disappointment in service. Relatively complex to maintain, it was equipped with radar and weapons that proved unable to match the performance of US types being fielded by Iran. Losses were heavy, and few positive results were achieved (*authors' collection*)

During Operation *Night Harvest*, initiated in the early 1980s, various US agencies were ordered to find ways of obtaining examples of aircraft operated by existing and potential enemies. In Iran, where the IRIAF was manned by a large number of US-trained personnel, this operation was highly successful, and led to a series of defections in which three Phantom IIs and a Tomcat were flown to Iraq in August and September 1986. Rumours then spread that an Iranian Tomcat had been flown to the USSR, although this never actually happened. Evidence for the success of *Night Harvest* came in March 2003 when US troops captured Tallil air base in southern Iraq and found the battered hulk of this Iranian F-4E (probably 3-6652). The remaining two Phantom IIs and the Tomcat that had defected were taken to Saudi Arabia by the Americans and subsequently destroyed (*US DoD via authors*)

Despite the Iranians experiencing great difficulty in keeping their F-14 fleet operational, they achieved outstanding results with the complex aircraft, which they maintained without any significant US support from late 1978 onwards. The IRIAF's 'Self-Sufficiency Jihad Team', the 7th and 8th TFW and IACI invested immense resources in maintaining the Tomcats. Although not obvious to outsiders, their efforts were clearly successful in the fact that the jet remains at the heart of the IRIAF's frontline force today. 3-6067 is seen here in front of the IACI compound at Mehrabad air base (*authors' collection*)

sensitive equipment had been removed. Then all the IRIAF markings were oversprayed with US stars and bars.

'The aircraft were then flown to Dhahran, in Saudi Arabia, for a proper study, where they were taken apart. They Americans examined each and every part, and many were taken away for study in the US. What was left of the jets was then crushed and blown up at a RSAF bombing range. All reports that we delivered F-14As or AIM-54s to the USSR are erroneous. Even years later, when Soviet officers arrived in Iran as MiG-29 and Su-24 instructors and asked us to fly our fighters, we wouldn't let them anywhere near our F-5s, let alone the F-14s.'

Two months later, on 7 December 1986, the Pentagon's Joint Intelligence Group, along with the CIA, top Grumman engineers and a large group of US Navy engineers and technicians, started a two-week meeting at the Foreign Technologies Laboratories – this is a highly classified Pentagon division, which usually works with the FTD. At the meeting, a list of 132 F-14 parts was presented, along with nine cases of actual Iranian Tomcat parts. The objective of the meeting was to determine whether Iran was capable of manufacturing spare parts, or if they were being produced elsewhere. The general conclusion was that Iran was manufacturing spares for its F-14 fleet.

In fact, the so-called 'Self-sufficiency Jihad' directorate of the IRIAF, IACI and engineers at the 'Communications Centre' of the Ministry of Posts, Telegraph and Telephones had started producing simpler F-14 parts in 1982. The first F-14 overhaul was completed in October of the same year. Several years later IRIAF technicians started replacing certain AWG-9 items with solid-state electronics. Such replacements actually resulted in the radar unit being lightened by six pounds (14 kg).

Initially, IRIAF pilots showed a reluctance to fly the modified aircraft, and even today some refuse to accept that such modifications had been carried out. This reluctance forced commanders and technical staff to deceive pilots by not telling them about the modifications. Once in the

air, however, they would be asked to change either the power output, working mode or frequency of the radar. To their surprise, crews would discover that their AWG-9 was now more powerful, and that its range had been increased.

Another ambitious F-14-related project was initiated in mid 1984 when the IRIAF command became concerned about depleting stocks of AIM-54s. Gen Compani ordered Col Mehdiyoun to prepare a study into a possible replacement, preferably by finding another long-range air-to-air missile system that would be available 'off-the-shelf' on the black market. The study, known within the IRIAF as *Long Fang*, concluded that there was nothing available in sufficient numbers in Iran, or elsewhere, other than the MIM-23 HAWK SAM. Iran had a large number in service, and continued to import additional rounds from Israel, Greece, Taiwan and South Korea right up until 1987.

While details about the project remain sketchy, the end result of this feasibility study was the commencement of Project *Sky Hawk* in 1985. It was run by Col Delhamed, whose younger brother had been killed by the Iraqis while flying an F-5E, and Maj Fazilat. Both were IRIAF technical officers. They received help from the 82nd TFS at Esfahan's TFB 8, and from a team of former IDF/AF technicians which included Pinkus Schepmsky, Danuta Laszuk and Avraham Wein.

The latter trio had already worked on a similar project in Israel in the late 1970s called *Distant Thunder* or *Distant Reach* in which the IDF/AF had tried to adapt the AGM-78 Standard anti-radiation missile to make F-4Es capable of confronting high and fast-flying MiG-25s and Tu-22s. The project was cancelled after the IDF/AF received F-15 Eagles armed with advanced AIM-7F missiles. The Israeli team was in Iran for 87 days, and in that time it had only limited access to one F-14A. They were also barred from attending live firing tests.

The complexity of this undertaking should not be underestimated, for the MIM-23 and F-14 were not really compatible. But after many studies, and several attempts, a HAWK was finally test-fired from a Tomcat in April 1986. During the testing, however, the capabilities of the AWG-9's data-link and the MIM-23's ability to convert AWG-9 radar signals proved weak.

More trials were undertaken with the two Tomcats adapted to carry HAWKs (renamed Sedjil in its new air-to-air role) on wing shoulder pylons. One or two rounds were even fired in combat, but *Sky Hawk* was effectively abandoned after the war. The IRIAF was to continue using the Phoenix missile as the Tomcat's main long-range weapon, and the problem of depleted stocks was later solved by other means.

This photograph of F-14A 3-6073 of the 82nd TFS was taken during early testing for Project *Sky Hawk*. The jet carries a MIM-23B I-HAWK round on its shoulder pylon in place of an AIM-54. During the test flights, an F-4E Phantom II of the 13th FS 'Fighter Instructors' performed the role of chase aircraft. The I-HAWK installation was carried out at Mehrabad air base, and the tests proved that the missile could only be fitted on the shoulder pylons. The long-range flight-testing and live-missile firings for Project *Sky Hawk* were carried out at Esfahan TFB. Aside from the 13th FS F-4, several C-130s from the 71st TTS were also gainfully employed during the project (*authors' collection*)

During the test-firing of I-HAWKs from F-14s, the Iranians soon learned that if the missile was to have any hope of scoring a hit, the Tomcat had to fly at no less than 10,000 ft and Mach 0.75, with the target at between 30,000 and 50,000 ft. Test-firings had to be carefully conducted, and although there are two claims for Iraqi fighters shot down by MIM-23s fired from F-14s, they remain unconfirmed (*authors' collection*)

When photographs like this appeared in western publications in 1998–99 they caused some surprise. Several reports claimed that the IRIAF was introducing the MIM-23 as an air-to-air missile on its F-14s. In fact, all of the these images were taken during Project *Sky Hawk* in 1986. While it is known that the IRIAF keeps Sedjils in its arsenal, many have been re-built as Yassers, incorporating the MIM-23B body and guidance system and the warhead of the M-117 bomb. The weapon is carried on the forward fuselage *(authors' collection)*

F-14As 3-6060 and 3-6079 conduct a test flight during Project *Sky Hawk*. Tomcats 3-6034 and 3-6073 were also used, and all four jets belonged to the 82nd TFS *(authors' collection)*

Project *Sky Hawk* was discontinued soon after the war with Iraq ended. According to former IRIAF officers, it was not particularly successful, as the data-link between the AWG-9 radar and the missile proved too weak. The I-HAWK's ability to convert radar signals from the AWG-9 was also criticised. Nevertheless, some additional testing of Sedjil missiles was done in the 1990s. This particular round was displayed by the IRIAF during the 'Holy War of Defence' exhibition, held in Tehran in November 2001 *(authors' collection)*

Yet depite the 'Self-sufficiency Jihad' of the early 1980s, production of many special and sensitive parts was only initiated in Iran a decade later. For this reason, the IRIAF's Tomcat fleet continued to suffer from a shortage of spare parts until the end of the war.

A mechanical failure may have caused the loss of the F-14 flown by Capt Gholamreza Assl-e-Davtalab and an unidentified RIO on 15 January 1987, the jet crashing near Izeh, in northern Khuzestan, killing the crew. It is not known if the aircraft was engaged in combat at the time of its demise.

F-14 – YALLA! YALLA!

Despite the stand-down caused by defections, IRIAF F-14 units were back in combat by early October 1986. They were then to see the most intensive and prolonged period of fighting of the whole conflict, being involved in over 150 air combats and claiming nearly 90 IrAF jets destroyed by war's end.

The 82nd TFS was successful on 6 October when an F-14A engaged a pair of Mirage F 1EQ-5s over the

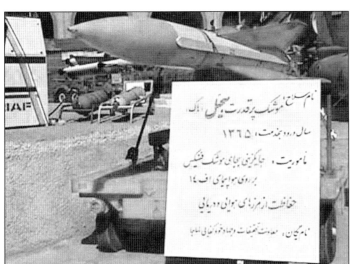

69

In addition to MiG-21RFs and MiG-25RBs, Mirage F 1EQs equipped with reconnaissance pods – like this example, carrying a COR-2 system – formed the main reconnaissance assets of the IrAF. An identically equipped F 1EQ provided the IRIAF with one of its first Mirage kills of the war in December 1981, the jet crashing off the Kuwaiti island of Bubiyan (*authors' collection*)

The IRIAF tried to keep 60 F-14s operational at any one time during the war with Iraq, these aircraft being split between three units and a detachment at Mehrabad. As the war ground on, this force level proved to be over-ambitious, and from 1986 the number of operational Tomcats dropped to slightly more than 30, of which only half were fully mission-capable. This greatly reduced number of available airframes put an additional strain on the remaining airworthy Tomcats, and their maintenance crews, but it meant that several airframes scored more than ten aerial victories – including 3-6067, seen here (*authors' collection*)

lower Persian Gulf shortly after an Exocet had hit the Greek tanker the *Faroship L*. A single AIM-54A destroyed one of the Mirages, and as the Tomcat closed on the second jet, the crew observed the F 1EQ-5 pilot flying over the spot where his leader had crashed into the sea. The F-14 turned to engage and the Iraqi panicked and flew into the water.

The following day, two Tomcats led by Capt A Afshar clashed with a large Iraqi strike force heading for Bushehr. Neither F-14 was armed with AIM-54s, the crews attacking with Sparrows and Sidewinders instead. Two Iraqi jets were shot down, but not before the tail of one of the Tomcats had been riddled with bullets – its pilot made an emergency landing at Bushehr. On 14 October a single F-14 intercepted eight Iraqis jets north of Khark and shot down a MiG-23 using an AIM-54A. Anxious to avoid a similar fate, the remaining fighters immediately turned around and headed home.

Yet despite these successes, foreign press reports continued to ignore the IRIAF and its F-14s, as Capt Rassi complained:

'So much was published about the IRIAF being "dead" or "finished off" after 1984. Some said it was not flying at all in 1986–87. But what nobody explained was why the Iraqis were buying so many SAMs and AAA pieces. They purchased no less than 18,000 heavy SAMs from the USSR and France during the war. By 1987 there were no fewer than 60 SAM sites in the Basra area alone. Why, if there was no threat?'

Maj Ali added:

'From 1987 onwards, the Western press reported that Iran no longer had a functioning air force. The truth was that we had problems maintaining the Tomcats, just like the US Navy. Serviceability in 1987 was lower than at any other time in the war, but does this mean we weren't flying and fighting? Even when the Americans maintained our Tomcats, they were less reliable and had higher maintenance requirements than our F-4s. It took 18 to 20 highly-trained technicians to maintain the F-14A properly, but only seven or eight to maintain the F-4E. For most of the war we had no more than 100 technicians fully qualified on the type.

'By June 1986, only 18 to 20 F-14s were combat ready, and only half had fully-operational AWG-9s. But from October large quantities of spare parts started arriving in Iran directly from the United States, allowing us to return between 30 and 35 F-14s to fully operational status once again. The fighting through the winter of 1986–87 was so intense, however, that by mid 1987 these spares had all been used up and the number of operational

aircraft had declined once more. This didn't mean we stopped flying. Although we had fewer operational aircraft, we kept them in the air longer. CAPs lasting up to 12 hours – the record was 13 – with the help of KC 707 tankers were normal.

'But if – as many say – our aircraft and AIM-54s weren't operational and we weren't flying, how did an F-14A crew use a Phoenix round to kill the son of IrAF Brig Gen Hekmat Abdul-Qadr? 1Lt Ahlan, died on 20 February 1987 when his Mirage F 1EQ was destroyed while escorting six Su-22 en route to

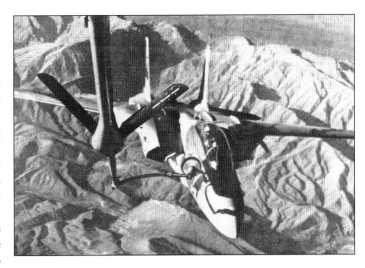

attack Iranian oil targets in the Persian Gulf. We had sent an F-4 into Iraqi airspace to act as bait, and when Ahlan and his wingman attempted to intercept it, they encountered two 81st TFS F-14As instead.

'The Tomcats were led by Capt Amiraslani, who had previously served as a highly respected 82nd TFS instructor. Only the second or third Iranian pilot to have ever fired an AIM-54A during training over Iran, he was forced out of the IIAF by the clerics during the revolution, but was allowed to return after war broke out. In short, Amiraslani was the perfect pilot for this kind of operation.

'When the Mirages started pursuing the lone Phantom II, which was then still inside Iraqi airspace, Amiraslani was on his CAP station east of the border. He fired one Phoenix at very long range and knocked down the lead Mirage flown by Ahlan. Over the radio, we heard the leader of the Iraqi Su-22 flight screaming, "F-Arba-Ashara! Yalla! Yalla!" In English that's, "F-14! Run! Run!" All six Sukhois and the sole surviving Mirage did just that. We recorded this message. In fact, we recorded many other things the Iraqis said on their radios.

'The Americans had trained us well, but still they said we weren't flying. So, when we weren't flying, why were the Iraqis running away from our F-14s? There's only one answer – they ran to live.'

Iran officially claimed three Iraqi Mirage F 1s shot down that day, in addition to several more damaged. IRIAF pilots later reported seeing Saudi helicopters flying SAR missions over the engagement area. A few days later, American Congressman Robert Torricelli, who had recently returned from a visit to Baghdad, said the IrAF had lost ten per cent of its aircraft in the previous two months.

More aerial clashes occurred in March, June, July and August, when the F-14s downed a MiG-23, several Mirages, an Su-22, an Exocet missile and a Super Frelon helicopter. The Tomcat force suffered another loss on 14 July 1987, however, when the F-14A flown by Maj Alireza Bitaraf crashed while fighting with at least 12 Iraqi jets.

The circumstances surrounding the jet's loss are unclear, some sources indicating that Bitaraf had suffered an engine stall during a dogfight over the Persian Gulf, and that the aircraft then fell into an unrecoverable flat spin at low level. This would not be surprising given the problems

A KC 707 tanker refuels 3-6027 over an Iranian mountain landscape in 1987. Note that the jet is carrying an AIM-54A Phoenix missile under the fuselage, but no Sidewinders or Sparrows. This indicates that the aircraft was probably on yet another 'Foxbat' hunt. Boeing 707-3J9C and Boeing 747-2J9C tankers were designated KC-707s and KC-747s in IRIAF service, but they were simply known as 'restaurants' to frontline fast jet crews (*authors' collection*)

Iranian Phantom IIs and Tomcats operated as closely together as possible during the war, and although it has been reported that the Tomcats were used as 'bait' for the F-4s, usually it was the latter which performed this role, with the F-14s as the hunters. This tactic was used to great effect on 20 February 1987, when the Mirage F 1EQ of 1Lt Ahlan was shot down by an AIM-54A while trying to catch an IRIAF F-4E Phantom II that had been sent his way as 'bait' (*Dassault via authors*)

experienced with the TF30, but Bitaraf was a seasoned Tomcat pilot who should have been able to deal with this situation. Other sources claim that his F-14 suffered a fuel system failure while returning from a test flight, and the jet crashed east of Esfahan as the pilot was attempting an emergency landing on a road.

On 29 August 1987 Maj Jalil Zandi downed a Mirage F 1EQ-5 over the lower Persian Gulf. The pilot ejected and was recovered by a US Navy warship. Two days later another Mirage was shot down and a second F 1 damaged – the latter was seen leaving the area in flames, trailing black smoke – after they had sunk the tanker *Bigorange XIV*. That same day Iranian intelligence sources state that Kuwaiti air defences also destroyed an IrAF combat aircraft when the pilot attempted to pass through its airspace on its way back to Iraq.

Following these losses – and also due to the pressure exerted on Baghdad by the US government – the Iraqis again stopped their attacks on supertankers in the Persian Gulf. They would not strike again for almost a month.

After better coordinating their operations with both the US Navy and the Saudis, the Iraqis hit a number of ships between Khark and Larak in late September and October. Passing over Kuwait, then along the Saudi coast, Iraqi Mirages F 1EQ-5s were able to reach deep into the Persian Gulf using two Antonov An-12BP tankers.

The IrAF enjoyed relative security due to the presence of USAF AWACS aircraft operating out of Saudi Arabia and US Navy warships patrolling the region – both would alert Iraqi pilots if IRIAF fighters were detected on radar. And in an emergency IrAF jets were permitted to divert to King Abdul Aziz air base near Dhahran to refuel, before returning home to Iraq.

Consequently, on a number of occasions intercepting Iranian F-14 pilots either failed to detect their opponents, or saw them jettisoning their ordnance and hastily escaping towards the south and west – in the opposite direction to Iraq!

In at least two cases, the Iraqis also flew far to the south, passing Qatar, before turning to attack Iranian oil installations on Larak and Hormuz. They were therefore able to take Iranian defences completely by surprise. Tomcat detachments were rapidly established at Bushehr to start flying CAPs in this area as well.

The IRIAF's badly depleted F-14 force was now stretched so thinly that it could not possibly cover all the strategically important areas in the Persian Gulf.

Maj Alireza Bitaraf and his RIO were lost on 14 July 1987 while battling with at least 12 Iraqi fighters, although the exact circumstances surrounding their deaths remains unclear (*authors' collection*)

The Iraqis started striking Iran's Persian Gulf oil rigs with Exocet missiles in 1986. US forces joined them in October 1987, usually 'in retaliation' for Iranian attacks on shipping during the 'tanker war'. This was one of the rigs shelled by US naval vessels that year

CRIPPLING THE WEASEL

Iranian aircrew not only fought Iraqis during the war with Iraq, but also pilots from other nationalities. Egyptians are known to have flown IrAF MiG-21s and MiG-23s at different times, while Belgians, South Africans, Australians and even a single American flew Mirage F 1EQs in 1985–86. In addition, French and Jordanian pilots acted as instructors, and while some flew combat missions, they apparently did not open fire.

There was additional Soviet and East German participation in Iraqi MiG-25 operations beyond that already mentioned. Although the Russian Defence Ministry's archive in Moscow has not yet released relevant documentation from the 1980s which would enable a complete study to be made of the involvement of Soviet instructors in the Iran–Iraq war, details are available from other sources. Interestingly, most reports that mention Soviet pilots stationed in Iraq state that they frequently encountered F-14s, and that several Russians were shot down. Usually only hand-picked, experienced Soviet pilots were chosen for such duties.

Soviet advisors had started to arrive in Iraq in significant numbers in the 1970s when Moscow had tried to become influential in local politics as a counter to Iran's close allegiance with the USA. Although such plans were frustrated by the ruling regime in Baghdad, more instructors were deployed to help the Iraqis operate the several hundred combat aircraft that the IrAF had ordered from the USSR in 1978.

Following a period during which the Soviet–Iraqi relationship cooled, the former started sending up-to-date equipment to Iraq for testing in

F-14A 3-6061 undertakes a training flight over Esfahan in 1986–87. After a pause of several years, the IRIAF started training new Tomcat crews at this time when replacements were urgently needed after six years of intensive fighting. Some pilots had been killed and others had left the service, but most survivors were simply exhausted. Nevertheless, the regime in Tehran was reluctant to let 'pro-Shah' pilots train new crews because of fears about their political influence. With their performance being closley scrutinised, instructors had to exercise great care while trying to pass on their extensive experience to newcomers. Meanwhile, the battle-proven pilots continued fighting, and between 21 and 27 February 1987, no less than five Iraqi Mirage F 1s were shot down by F-14s in two separate engagements over the Persian Gulf (*authors' collection*)

Although of poor quality, this photograph of 3-6020, taken in 1986, is nevertheless interesting because it shows that the Iranians started testing the 'Bombcat' concept years before the US Navy – examination of the load beneath this F-14 reveals two Mk 83 bombs. Mindful of its Tomcats' value, however, the IRIAF was reluctant to expose them to Iraqi air defences, preferring to use their bomb-hauling capability on limited occasions, such as for destroying key targets along the Iran/Iraq border. Of all the Iranian F-14As, 3-6020 was one of the most successful during the war. In addition to shooting down a MiG-21 and achieving a near-miss against a MiG-25RB on 15 May 1981, it is known to have scored more than a dozen other kills, as well as participating in the 'Bombcat' project. It survived the war and became the first IRIAF F-14A to receive the new camouflage colours after a major overhaul by IACI at Mehrabad (*authors' collection***)**

combat from 1981 onwards. These systems included MiG-27s armed with Kh-29T/L air-to-surface missiles, which arrived in Iraq in March 1985. The MiGs flew intensive operations in support of Iraqi counter-attacks against the Iranian *Fatima Zahra* Offensive, which had seen troops push deep into Iraq and cut off Highway 6 linking Basra to al-Amarah.

The Soviet MiG-27 detachment comprised ten pilots and a similar number of aircraft. Flying two combat sorties daily, they hit Iranian positions particularly hard with the Kh-29s. As usual, the Iranians responded swiftly to the new threat and started deploying their interceptors in the area to ambush the MiGs. The operation was instantly successful, with three Soviet-flown MiG-27s being shot down by AIM-54s and a fourth falling to an AIM-9P fired from an F-4E. All three pilots from the aircraft hit by Phoenix missiles were killed, while the fourth survived – he was recovered in a Combat-SAR mission involving no less than 12 IrAF fighter aircraft and 20 IrAAC helicopters. The Soviet unit was immediately returned to the USSR.

Another type tested extensively by the Soviets in Iraq was the MiG-25BM 'Wild Weasel' version of the 'Foxbat', examples of which were deployed to H-3 for several weeks in 1986. Not much is known about their activities, except that they ended abruptly when one was shot down by an F-14A using a Phoenix when it attempted to dash back across the Iraqi border at high altitude and top speed.

In November 1987 the MiG-25BM was given a second chance when four brand-new examples – together with pilots from the 98th and the 164th Reconnaissance Wings – were deployed to H-3, along with 130 technicians, support equipment and spare parts. Weapons supplied for use with the aircraft comprised Kh-58U (AS-11) and Kh-25MP (AS-12) anti-radar missiles (ARMs). The purpose of the deployment was to test the MiG-25BMs' ECM systems against IRIAF F-14s, and also to try out their Kh-58Us against Iranian MIM-23B batteries.

The first mission was flown from Samarah air base on the night of 8 November, the 'Foxbats'' target being Mehrabad air base, which at the time was protected by two MIM-23B I-HAWK SAM batteries. Fifteen Phoenix-armed F-14As were also based there. This raid, and one which followed a day later, saw all the jets flown by Soviet pilots, and they appeared to have been successful. The MiG-25BMs proved capable of operating at up to 68,900 ft with impunity, and they also disabled at least one Iranian radar site near Mehrabad. But the third mission, flown on the night of 11 November, was to end rather differently.

Shortly after entering Iranian airspace, the MiG-25BM was intercepted by an F-14, which fired a single AIM-54 in HOJ (Home-On-Jamming) mode despite severe jamming. The missile guided flawlessly, but the warhead failed to explode. Nevertheless, the Phoenix clipped the target's fin and the Soviet pilot had no choice but to crash-land on the nearest landing strip in Iraq, destroying the aircraft in the process. To the embarrassment of the Soviet government, and its air force, and in the full view of US reconnaissance satellites, the wrecked 'Foxbat' was loaded into an Il-76 transport and flown to the USSR. Four days later, the Soviet personnel at H-3 packed their equipment and left.

The MiG-25BMs were to return to Iraq, however, in July 1988. This time, their mission was to test upgraded Kh-58Us and Kh-31P ARMs against Iranian Westinghouse ADS-4 low-band and long-range early-warning radars. At least one successful mission was flown against the Subashi early-warning radar site near Hamedan, two missiles destroying the radar and inflicting heavy losses among highly experienced operators.

DEFENDING KHUZESTAN

In November 1987, simultaneously with the Soviet MiG-25BM testing, the IrAF started a counter-air offensive against Iranian air bases in Khuzestan. This was to initiate a phase of vicious air battles which were to last until the end of the war, and cost both sides dearly.

On 15 November, for example, an F-14A flown by Maj Afkhami intercepted a formation of Mirage F 1EQs over Gachsaran, in the northern Persian Gulf. Using AIM-7s, he claimed one jet shot down and another damaged. The IRIAF actually credited him with two confirmed kills for reasons still unknown, taking his tally to seven kills – five confirmed and two probables. Afkhami was known within the 8th TFW as a 'solid' pilot, and a CO who pushed his men hard to get the job done.

It was at this time that the availability of the IRIAF's F-14A fleet fell to an unprecedented level, with only 15 jets being fully mission-capable on average. An additional 20 airframes were flyable, but their AWG-9s were not working. The stock of AIM-54s was also low, with less than 50 operational rounds being available due to a chronic shortage of thermal batteries. These batteries could only be purchased in the USA, and they would cost the Iranians up to $10,000 apiece when they finally found a clandestine buyer that could source them. The next shipment of thermal batteries for AIM-54s was not to arrive in Iran until 1990.

The small number of operational Tomcats and AIM-54s had to be carefully husbanded, therefore, and were only used to defend strategically important areas such as Khark or Tehran. Yet, the US Navy's growing presence in the Persian Gulf and the Sea of Oman forced the Iranians to disperse their Tomcats – especially fully operational ones – even more thinly by deploying several to Bandar Abbas. It was at this time that the IrAF was unleashed to deliver the 'final blow' against Khark, as well as the supertankers using the facility. Maj Ali recalled:

'The IrAF was very active in February 1988, flying many raids against our tankers. Then they escalated the situation by launching simultaneous offensives against Khark and other installations deeper inside the Persian Gulf on which we depended for exporting our oil. Attacks on our tankers were meaningless because we had plenty of them, but raids against Khark, Larak and other loading installations could not be tolerated.'

The IrAF's newly formed 115th Sqn, equipped with the first of 12 Mirage F 1EQ-6s, now initiated a kind of mini-war against the 81st TFS

The excellent view from the cockpit of the F-14A – well illustrated by this photograph of 3-6067 – was much appreciated by Iranian fighter pilots. The ability to see clearly around the aircraft was extremely important in air combat, especially when F-14s flying alone, or in pairs, engaged much larger Iraqi formations. 3-6067 is known to have participated in several such battles, and was credited with at least 11 aerial kills. Seen here with its refuelling probe extended, the jet was photographed on display at an exhibition in Tehran in the late 1980s (*authors' collection*)

by challenging the Tomcats over the Persian Gulf. This version of the Mirage was to become the most dangerous opponent encountered by the Tomcats during the war. It was equipped with the latest version of the Cyrano IV radar, which was compatible with the Matra Super 530D medium-range air-to-air missile. This weapon was originally designed for the Mirage 2000, and up to 30 trial rounds were secretly supplied to Iraq in January 1988, together with 80 improved Matra R 550 Magic Mk II missiles with 'all-aspect' capabilities. The Iraqis also introduced new ECM systems in an effort to counter the AWG-9, as Capt Javad explained:

'The Iraqis, the French and the Soviets had tried everything possible to jam our AWG-9s, thus revealing just how much they feared our Tomcats. Testing one system after another, they tried deception jamming, barrage jamming, spot jamming and overload jamming, but nothing worked.

'What made the AWG-9 so resistant was its high basic radar frequency, as well as its frequency agility. If they tried to jam us, we simply switched the frequency, while the radar itself rejected signals that didn't conform to the precise pattern of its scan. We seldom encountered any problems, and when we did, they usually occurred when we tried to employ the AIM-7. The AIM-54s showed no vulnerability to ECM whatsoever.'

Due to repeated French efforts to sell Mirage F 1s to Iran, the IRIAF was very familiar with the jet's capabilities, and the performance of its weapons, including the Super 530D/F missiles. Consequently, the Tomcat crews had little difficulty in evading them.

The growing support for Iraqi operations by US Navy vessels, and aircraft, operating within the Persian Gulf was more difficult to deal with, however. On occasion, the Americans not only supplied targeting information to the IrAF, but also warned Iraqi pilots of the presence of IRIAF fighters and jammed Iranian early warning radar. This made it difficult for the Iranians to prevent strikes on their ships and facilities.

The first major engagement of this period took place on 9 February 1988 when, at 0930 hrs, the IRIAF early warning site at Kohkilooyeh detected Iraqi fighters approaching a convoy of tankers heading for Khark. Two F-14As were immediately scrambled, one of which was flown by 1Lt (now Lt Col) Qiyassi – he had emerged as the best pilot from the first class of IRIAF F-14 crews trained in Iran after the start of the war.

Only Qiyassi's Tomcat engaged the Iraqis, but it was enough. GCI guided the pilot southwards, and then instructed the RIO to sweep the area with the AWG-9. Six Mirages were detected, and at 1011 hrs battle was joined. Qiyassi fired his first Sparrow from a range of 5.5 miles (10 km), and the AIM-7E-4 guided flawlessly and scored a direct hit, sending the F 1EQ-5 down in flames. The pilot then noticed two more Mirages closing on him from either side, one from the left and one from the right. Diving to a lower altitude, they then turned sharply to the right. Both jets were identified as Mirage F 1EQ-5s due to their dark sea grey camouflage applied for over-water operations.

Turning behind the Iraqis, Qiyassi noticed that one of them had made the fatal mistake of reversing to the left, thus exposing the rear of his jet to the F-14. Seconds later Qiyassi attempted to fire a Sidewinder, but the missile malfunctioned. Selecting the next AIM-9P, the pilot watched with satisfaction as the missile flew right up the tailpipe of the Mirage. The French fighter disintegrated.

In 1987 and early 1988, the IrAF conducted a campaign of terror against Iranian civilians living along the border with Iraq. Many villages, towns and cities were attacked with bombs and missiles. This photograph shows the school at Mianeh, in northern Iran, which received at least one direct hit during an Iraqi attack in 1988, killing more than 60 teachers and children. Having been ignored by the new Iranian regime after the 1979 revolution, the IRIAF came under heavy pressure from the Mullahs, as well as the public, to protect these border towns following such attacks (*authors' collection*)

Operating without aerial refuelling support, Qiyassi now decided to return to Bushehr. One hour later the same crew scrambled again, and when they reached 20,000 ft they made several wide sweeps with the AWG-9 but found nothing. Then, while turning back towards the southeast, two contacts were detected at a range of 16 km (ten miles). Again, there was no time for an engagement with AIM-54s, so Qiyassi selected afterburner and dived straight at the Iraqi jets.

Spotting the lone Tomcat, the IrAF Mirage F 1s scattered in all directions as they tried to shake the pursuer off by flying at high speed and low level over the sea. This move proved to be unsuccessful, however, as after only one turn the F-14 was already behind them. At 1242 hrs Qiyassi fired an AIM-9P, but with another Mirage dangerously close behind him, he was forced to break – he was unable to see the end result of his attack. After making several more turns to ascertain that no Mirages were behind him, Qiyassi returned to the spot where he had fired his Sidewinder. Finding only burning wreckage on the surface of the water, his kill was confirmed by sailors aboard several ships in a nearby convoy. Qiyassi was awarded five gold coins for his success, which he donated to the war effort.

This clash was one of only a handful of aerial engagements publicised in Iran during the war, and it included a rare TV interview with the crew. This success was greeted with disbelief in the West at the time, as few observers believed that IRIAF F-14s were still operational, or that their pilots were capable of such a feat. But this was only one in a series of battles that occurred in early 1988.

HUNTING THE HUNTERS

Despite the loss of two Mirages, the IrAF's F 1EQs were back searching for targets to attack just days later, and on 15 February two struck the oil-loading terminal on Sirri Island. Despite their attack being covered by nearby US Navy ships, and their jets boasting sophisticated RWRs, both pilots were caught off guard by a lone 81st TFW F-14A. It fired a single Phoenix from very long range and destroyed a Mirage.

Legendary Iranian F-14 pilot Maj A Rahnavard scored heavily in February 1988. Another 'Shah's Pilot', he was qualified to fly F-4s, F-5s, F-14s and C-130s, and had somehow survived the purge of the 81st TFW in the year following the revolution. Rahnavard mainly flew Phantom IIs and Tomcats during the war, and was initially only permitted to crew the jets as a WSO/RIO. However, as the demand for good F-14 pilots rose in late 1986, he was allowed back into the front seat. Viewed by his peers as a very good Tomcat pilot, Rahnavard never achieved 'acedom', although he was considered a 'Top Gun' within the IRIAF. He was respected not only for his air-to-air kills, but also, in the words of his former colleagues, 'because of his great heart and bravery against all odds'.

On the morning of 16 February 1988, Rahnavard was flying a lone F-14A on a CAP some 23 km (14 miles) west of Khark when his RIO detected two groups of four Iraqi fighters heading straight for them. They were closing simultaneously from several different directions, and Rahnavard recognised that his opponents were employing a standard tactic used by the Iraqis to overwhelm IRIAF Tomcats. He countered by firing a single Sparrow before they could press home their attack. The first missile malfunctioned, however, and fell into the sea.

Sensing that his remaining AIM-7s were probably also useless, Rahnavard selected 'HEAT' instead. Climbing and then breaking, he dived out of the sun and latched onto the tails of the nearest pair of Mirages. Hearing a good tone, Rahnavard fired a Sidewinder and watched as his target turned into a brilliant fireball.

Despite losing one of their number, the Mirage pilots had accomplished their mission of drawing the Tomcat away from an inbound strike package. In the seconds that followed, the latter formation entered the IRIAF air defence zone around Khark. Knowing there was little he could do, Rahnavard decided to withdraw to the north and refuel from a waiting KC 707. He still had three functional Sidewinders, and he intended to put them to good use.

Over Khark, the Iraqis flew straight into the air defence killing zone, and the lead Mirage F 1EQ fell to an MIM-23B. To their credit, the IrAF pilots pressed home their attacks, delivering their bombs with precision. But as they started their return journey, Rahnavard was thundering northwards at high speed and low level. Encountering the Iraqis once again, he attacked an F 1 from the rear with an AIM-9P. Initially alarmed as he saw the missile head for the sea, Rahnavard's despair changed to elation as his missile homed in on its target and hit the jet's rear fuselage, causing it to crash into the water. Following this loss, the IrAF did not return to Khark for nine days. The F-14s were waiting for them.

At 1855 hrs on 25 February, Capt G Esmaeli intercepted an Iraqi Xian B-6D bomber seconds after it had launched a C 601 anti-ship missile at an Iranian warship. Esmaeli and his RIO ripple fired two AIM-54As and shot down both the B-6D and the C 601.

February 1988 had been a highly successful month for the 81st TFS. Its pilots were credited with five confirmed and two probable Mirage F 1EQ-5/6 kills, plus the B-6D destroyed. The two probables had been scored during the first aerial battle in which the squadron had

In the autumn of 1987, four Xian B-6D bombers (licence-built Tupolev Tu-16s) were supplied to the IrAF's 8th Bomber Squadron by China. Dubbed the ultimate 'tanker hunters', and armed with C 601 anti-ship missiles, they became operational in early 1988. Patrolling the commercial corridors in the lower Persian Gulf, where they posed a threat to tankers even in the Straits of Hormuz, the B-6Ds proved to be difficult targets. One was intercepted and shot down by an F-14A on 25 February 1988, however, after which they never ventured beyond Bahrain (*authors' collection*)

suffered its first actual combat loss of the entire war. The IRIAF's ranking ace, Maj Jalil Zandi, had put up a tremendous fight against eight Mirages, scoring hits on two opponents (it is not clear if they went down, as the crew had no time to track their Sidewinders), before his Tomcat was hit by several R 550s and a single Super 530D. Somehow, the pilot managed to extract his badly damaged aircraft from the engagement and head back to Iran, where its sole remaining engine quit and the crew had to eject.

This was Zandi's last combat sortie of the war, by which time he had nine confirmed and three probable kills to his credit, making him the highest-scoring F-14 pilot of the war. Despite having flown the Tomcat pre-revolution, Zandi was to enjoy a successful career with the IRIAF post-war. He retired in 2001 with the rank of lieutenant general, but died soon afterwards due to heart failure.

PHOENIX AT WORK

The 81st TFS was to enjoy more success in March 1988 as well, although the first kill that month was actually scored by the 82nd TFS, which shot down an Su-20 during an engagement over western Iran on the 1st – the downed Iraqi pilot, 1Lt Samir Naji Nosayef, was captured. On the 18th, a 81st TFS F-14A destroyed another Mirage F 1EQ-5 over the Persian Gulf in full view of several US Navy warships. The unit achieved its greatest success the following day when the IrAF, emboldened by US Navy reports that the waters between Khark and Bushehr looked like 'a shooting gallery' full of 'excellent targets' for Exocets, made its greatest ever effort to stop Iranian oil exports from Khark.

At around 0100 hrs on 19 March, the first Iraqi wave, consisting of four Tu-22Bs and six Mirages, took of from Shoaibah air base, near Basra. This strike was devastating. Two of the Mirages launched their Exocets, scoring two hits in the accommodation block of the tanker *Kyrnicos* and damaging the ship so badly that it had to be towed back to Larak Island. Then, 32 minutes later, and supported by heavy jamming from escorting Mirages fitted with Caiman ECM pods, more Tu-22 'Blinders' struck with 12 FAB-500 bombs apiece.

The bombers arrived over the island completely unannounced and hit the 316,398-ton supertanker *Ava'i* with several bombs, which caused a major conflagration. Massive explosions ripped the giant vessel apart, killing 22 of its crew. Nearby, the 253,837-ton *Sanandaj* was also hit with equal precision. The ship was gutted by fire and 26 crewmen perished. The 'Blinders' disappeared before even a single IRIAF interceptor could scramble from Bushehr.

US Navy vessels sailing nearby monitored the attack and reported that it was executed in good order. But some American officers who watched it called the Iraqi operation 'deplorable in nature', and ships in the area were ordered to stop supporting the Iraqis. This order was given just as the second IrAF wave of two Tu-22Bs, four MiG-25RBs, six MiG-23BKs and

A Tu-22B of the IrAF's 7th Bomber Squadron, 10th Composite Bomber Wing after its refurbishment in the USSR. In addition to Mirages and MiG-25s, Tomcat pilots particularly relished the prospect of engaging Iraqi Tu-22s. Opportunities were few, and in the first four years of the war only three of these fast and effective bombers were shot down by the F-14s. The fourth, and last, Tu-22B to be destroyed by the Tomcat force was claimed on 18 March 1988 when 8th TFW pilots delivered a decisive blow against the Iraqi 'Strategic Brigade', as the 10th Wing was sometimes known within the IrAF (*authors' collection*)

two Su-22M4-Ks was approaching Khark from the north-west. This time, two IRIAF F-14As were heading for Khark from the south-east and two F-4Es from the south.

What happened when these aircraft met over Khark at 0932 hrs that morning can only be described as a complete catastrophe for the IrAF, even if the exact details remain sketchy. The F-14 crews worked well as a pair, and they were fortunate in that their jets were in operational condition. US Navy

warships recorded that several AIM-54s were launched, resulting in the downing of at least one Tu-22B and one MiG-25RB. Minutes later the F-4Es destroyed another Tu-22B with AIM-7Es. It is probable that other Iraqi bombers were also shot down, but this remains unconfirmed.

While the Tomcats were engaging the Iraqi bombers high above Khark, the MiG-23s and Su-22s pressed home their attack at low level. The sole MIM-23B SAM site was alerted and ready, and it fired several HAWKs in quick succession which were later confirmed as having destroyed at least one MiG and a single Sukhoi just 30 seconds apart.

The strike which caused the loss of the supertankers was certainly the heaviest and – for both sides – the costliest of the whole 'tanker war'. The Iraqis had destroyed two of Iran's largest ships, which were used for transporting crude oil to the lower Persian Gulf for loading into customers' vessels. Their destruction caused considerable delay to Iranian oil exports. On the other hand, the IrAF not only failed to destroy the oil installations once again, but also lost at least two Tu-22Bs and a single MiG-25RB, MiG-23BK and Su-22M-4K, with their irreplaceable crews.

The 1st FRS, IrAF was to suffer two further losses within a short period. On 20 March, four MiGs flew into Iranian airspace, splitting their formation into two pairs. At 1412 hrs two 'Foxbats' reached Boroujerd, while the other two bombed Hamedan eight minutes later, killing 25 civilians and injuring 46 others. Two minutes earlier, however, one of the

An IRIAF F-14A crew completes a pre-flight check in early 1988. Note the AIM-9P Sidewinder mounted on the port wing shoulder pylon, and the AIM-7E-4 Sparrow immediately below it. While the AIM-9 is usually described as the best short-range air-to-air missile of the war, Iranian experience with the AIM-7 matched that of US pilots in Vietnam, who found that the weapon sometimes functioned well, but on other occasions was totally useless. But unlike American pilots, the Iranians never used the AIM-7 in dogfights. It was employed exclusively in medium-range engagements, being fired from a forward aspect at a range of 12 km (seven miles). While most pilots remained unimpressed with the AIM-7, careful handling and precise pre-flight checks assured a kill probability of more than 20 per cent – twice that achieved in Vietnam (*authors' collection*)

In the autumn of 1987, the IrAF started introducing Su-22UM3-K/M-4K fighter bombers into service. These represented the first version of this venerable fighter to be compatible with precision-guided munitions, and their main task was SEAD (suppression of enemy air defences). The type suffered heavy losses to Iranian interceptors, although it proved capable of jamming the radars of F-4s and F-5s, and attacked MIM-23 SAM sites with Kh-28/AS-9 anti-radar missiles – an example of the latter can be seen in the foreground. The F-14 had no problem dealing with any Iraqi SEAD aircraft, and even downed two Soviet-flown MiG-25BMs using AIM-54s (*authors' collection*)

MiGs was shot down near Boroujerd while turning for home. On 22 March, two MiG-25RBs bombed Tabriz. Again, one aircraft was shot down at 1630 hrs, crashing in the mountains that surrounded the city. Finally, another Mirage was destroyed on the 24th.

Although the Iran–Iraq War was now coming to an end, there was no shortage of aerial action, as Maj Ali explained:

'While the West and Iraq claimed that virtually no Iranian Tomcats – at best only a dozen or so – were left operational in Iran, a sort of "mini-war" developed between us and Iraqi Mirage F 1EQ-5/6 units from February until July 1988. For most of the war, the Iraqis ran away, but now F 1 pilots started to engage us head-to-head. They were well trained by the Soviets and French and were the most aggressive I'd encountered during the war. Their tactics was sound and their attacks well planned.

'Their F 1EQ-5/6s were the best fighters they had, closely comparable to our F-4s in capability, especially with their new weapons. We didn't fear them – even the best Iraqi pilot was not as good as our average ones – but we respected them. We never ran even if outnumbered eight-to-one, and when the best tactic would have been to disengage.'

This was confirmed during the two battles fought by the IRIAF's F-14s in May and June 1988. In mid May Capt A Afshar scored his fifth kill when he downed a Mirage F 1EQ near Tehran. This was followed on 9 July by the war's final F-14 kill. Capt Rassi reported:

'We were aware of the Super 530Fs and well informed about them. We had no problems staying out of their envelope, as on 9 July, when Maj Zooghi shot down a Mirage escorting a group of Su-22s over Abadan. But the Super 530D, with its longer range, Mach 5+ speed and better snap-down capability, was a nasty surprise.

'On 19 July 1988, four Mirage F 1EQ-6s approached a pair of our F-14s. They converged on them from different directions, jamming our fighters so as to deny them the opportunity to use their AIM-54s. They then engaged with Super 530D missiles. Both Tomcats were downed. Some 20 minutes later the Mirages came back and shot down an F-4E that we had sent out to locate the downed crews. Our HQs then told us that the missiles used by the Mirages had homed on radar emissions from our AWG-9s. Only later did we learn that the French had supplied a trial batch of their Super 530Ds to Iraq.'

And so the IrAF, after suffering immense losses to Iranian F-14s during the long and bloody war, ended the conflict on a high note. And the tired IRIAF F-14 pilots were denied an opportunity to respond in kind.

During the last year of the war, Iraqi Mirages (represented here by F 1EQ-6 4622) posed the greatest threat to the Iranian Tomcats. IRIAF pilots knew how good most of the late-war Iraqi Mirage pilots were because of their French training and their high level of experience. During repeated clashes with F-14s, however, IrAF pilots learned that being experienced, bold and courageous was not enough. Up to 30 Mirage F 1EQs and one Mirage 5 are known to have been shot down by Iranian F-14s for the loss of three Tomcats (*authors' collection*)

THE FOG OF DISINFORMATION

It remains unclear exactly how many air-to-air kills were scored by IRIAF F-14s between 7 September 1980 and 7 July 1988, as Air Force records were repeatedly tampered with during and after the war, mainly for political, religious or personal reasons. This has led to considerable confusion.

Post-war, a conference that was held in Tehran, and attended by commanders from all branches of the participating military and paramilitary forces, concluded that the IRIAF had fired a total of 71 AIM-54As and had lost ten more rounds when the F-14s carrying them had either crashed, defected or were shot down. This figure may be correct, although the conference also determined that the F-14s had scored just 30 kills during the war. Of this figure, 16 were confirmed as having been achieved by AIM-54As, with four probables, one destroyed by a Sparrow, with two probables and seven confirmed by Sidewinders.

The evidence presented included reports from pilots of both sides, gun-camera/TISEO films and photographs of wreckage, plus foreign and domestic intelligence reports. The conference credited almost 70 per cent of the kills scored in aerial combat by IRIAF fighters – particularly those by F-14s – to IRGC air defence units, or disallowed them altogether. And this conclusion was reached despite firm evidence existing for 130 confirmed and 23 probable kills by IRIAF F-14As. Of those, at least 40 were scored with AIM-54s, two or three with guns, around 15 with AIM-7s and the rest with AIM-9s. In one instance, four Iraqi fighters were shot down by a single Phoenix, and there were two cases of two Iraqi fighters being destroyed by the same missile.

More importantly, the Tomcat provided the ultimate deterrence against marauding IrAF fighter-bombers. Not only did it down many Iraqi jets, it forced many more to abort their missions before

Tomcat 3-6020 performs a low level fly past of Khark Island in the late 1990s. Keeping the Tomcats operational throughout the long Iran-Iraq War bolstered morale within the IRIAF, and maintained a competitive spirit between units flying other types. And although Iranian F-4 and F-5 pilots sometimes criticised their F-14 brethren for behaving as if they could fight the war on their own, all realised the Tomcat's significance to Iran (*authors' collection*)

The development of new polyurethane-based paint which was applied to IRIAF F-14As from 1995 onwards caused some sources in the West to claim that Iranian Tomcats had now been camouflaged in a 'radar-absorbing' scheme. As can be seen from this photograph, the paint possesses no special qualities. Also visible in this view of 3-6024's left fin is the jet's TFB number and the Iranian flag, which has been applied to all IRIAF aircraft since 1979. Finally, note the aircraft's BuNo beneath the stabilator (*authors' collection*)

The right side view of the newly repainted 3-6024 shows the extended in-flight refuelling probe (without doors) and all the fuselage stencilling in English, and in the standard positions used by the US Navy. The ATM-54A Phoenix training round in the foreground was one of ten supplied to Iran in 1976 (*authors' collection*)

The left side of 3-6024, again showing cockpit area details (*authors' collection*)

reaching their targets. The simple fact was that where F-14s operated, there were no Iraqi fighters. As Maj Ali explained, no air defence system has ever proven so effective:

'In the West, many declared the F-14 and AIM-54 to be a very expensive "failure". Even if you take into account the total number of kills scored by the system against the Iraqis, questions could still be asked about the value of the effort to keep the labour-intensive Tomcats and AIM-54s operational, and the overall expense involved in doing so. However, when I look back at our service record with the jet I look beyond its exceptional performance as purely an interceptor. We used it to escort fighters and tankers and flew many radar-reconnaissance missions as "mini-AWACS" for the protection of others in the air and on the ground. We also intimidated the IrAF for much of the war without even firing a shot. To this you can add over 130 aerial kills. In the final analysis, the F-14/AIM-54 was anything but a "failure" in IRIAF service.'

Despite this record, IRIAF pilots were far from satisfied with the performance of the Tomcat's engines, as Capt Rassi recalled:

'The Tomcat was a good dogfighter and a formidable challenge to any Iraqi MiG or Mirage. But our F-14s had problems as well. The dwindling number of flyable airframes and never-ending engine problems kept us from becoming true hunter-killers and destroying everything that came our way. I never trusted the Tomcat's engines, for example. Just a small mistake with the throttle during a dogfight could end with an engine compressor stall. That usually meant a crash. By war's end, TF30s had destroyed far more of our F-14s than the Iraqis ever could. We had more Tomcats parked in underground shelters waiting for engine repairs than flyable examples. No Iranian pilot ever flew his F-14 without keeping an eye on the engine settings.'

Maj Nuzran summed up the capability of the Tomcat's weapons system and the AWG-9 radar:

'During the whole war, I never heard of the AWG-9 radar being successfully jammed. There were a handful of cases of radar lock-on being broken by close-range manoeuvring or by MiG-25s using their high speed to outrun an F-14, but the Iraqis (using French equipment) and the Soviets never managed to jam our radars. They expended considerable effort trying to do so, using different systems.

A TF30 undergoes engine runs in full afterburner on the proof stand at IACI. Although officially rated at 20,900 lbs thrust in full afterburner, the twin-spool, low-bypass ratio turbofan TF30 engine actually develops at least 22,000 lbs in certain conditions. As a pioneer in modern military propulsion technology, the TF30 was also the first turbofan equipped with afterburner (producing extra power in five so-called 'zones'), and the first engine to give an aircraft supersonic capability at sea level. Iranian F-14As are fitted with TF30-P-414As. Rumours about the re-equipment of Iranian F-14As with Russian-built avionics and engines have proved baseless to date. The aircraft continues to soldier on in its original configuration, although much of the F-14's avionics fit has been upgraded to modern standards. TF30s still power Iranian Tomcats, and there are no serious indications that this is about to change (*authors' collection*)

'They tried deception, barrage, spot and overload jamming, but they weren't successful. Our radars had a high basic working frequency and excellent frequency agility, so it was easy to move the radar away from jamming signals and reject those which didn't match the precise search pattern of our AWG-9. On several occasions they tried overwhelming us by combining all of these methods. I once detected 11 jets closing simultaneously on me using jamming, but this posed no great problem, as my AWG-9 could handle twice as many targets simultaneously. And my RIO and I solved the jamming problem within seconds.'

Capt Rassi pointed out that when the AWG-9 broke down, the cause was usually an inoperable Airborne Missile Control Computer (AMCC):

'This didn't mean we couldn't use an aircraft with a broken AMCC. We could still fly and fight, armed with Sidewinders and the Vulcan cannon. Our pilots scored many kills flying Tomcats under such conditions. Apart from INS systems and gyros, the component that grounded most of our F-14s had nothing to do with the AWG-9. The one for which Iran paid more than for any other on the black market was the Flight Data or Air Data Computer. This was the most vital of all the jet's "black boxes", and without it the F-14 couldn't fly, let alone fight.'

As with the controversy surrounding the exact number of kills claimed by the F-14, the precise number of losses suffered by the Tomcat force is also open to conjecture. If all known Iraqi war communiqués are to be trusted, more than 70 Iranian Tomcats were shot down between November 1982 and 19 July 1988! Many Western sources reported that three were lost in air combat, but they also claimed that the air war between Iraq and Iran was neither 'intensive' nor 'interesting'.

Basing reports on information released by the Foreign Broadcast Information System in Washington, DC, which supplied foreign media reports to various US authorities, Western, Russian and Ukrainian sources claim that the IRIAF lost 12 to 16 F-14s. Firm confirmation, however, exists only for three jets shot down in air combat with Iraqi fighters and four by (Iranian) SAMs. There are indications that two more were lost in combat in unknown circumstances and as many as seven in accidents, mainly due to engine or flight control failure or for reasons unknown. At least eight others were badly damaged but returned to service after the war.

A right side view of 3-6024, showing the details of its then new camouflage scheme. Note that even the upper part of the weapons pylon under the wing is painted light blue, and that the front section of the nose remains in 'radome tan' (*authors' collection*)

APPENDICES

IRANIAN F-14A TOMCAT VICTORIES

This list includes 159 confirmed kills, which have been sourced from active or retired Iranian F-14, F-4 and F-5 pilots, retired Iraqi MiG-21, Su-20/22 and Mirage F 1EQ pilots, official Iranian records, US Navy documents such as *Speartip* and third-hand sources such as press releases or 'war communiqués'. The list also includes 34 probable/possible or unconfirmed kills, with details from the same sources, and two claims for damaged Iraqi fighters. Within these figures are also three known firings against Iraqi anti-ship missiles – officially, none scored a hit, but unofficially at least the C 601 claimed on 25 February 1988 was shot down. Entries in bold type are based on unconfirmed information.

Date	Unit	Aircrew	Weapon	Victim/Air Force
7 Sep 80	81 TFS/TFB 8	withheld	20 mm	Mi-25, 4 ATTSOS/1W/IrAAC
10 Sep 80	TFB 8	?	AIM-9P	MiG-21R/IrAF
10 Sep 80	**TFB 8**	**?**	**AIM-7E-4**	**MiG-21/IrAF**
13 Sep 80	81 TFS/TFB 8	M-R Attaie	AIM-54A	MiG-23MS/IrAF
23 Sep 80	81 TFS/TFB 8	A Azimi	AIM-54A	MiG-21, RF 1 FRS/IrAF
23 Sep 80	**81 TFS/TFB 8**	**A Azimi**	**AIM-54A**	**MiG-23MS/IrAF**
23 Sep 80	81 TFS/TFB 8	?	AIM-7E-4	MiG-23/IrAF
23 Sep 80	81 TFS/TFB 8	?	AIM-7E-4	MiG-23/IrAF
23 Sep 80	81 TFS/TFB 8	?	AIM-9J	MiG-21/IrAF
24 Sep 80	81 TFS/TFB 8	N K	AIM-7E-4	MiG-21MF/IrAF
24 Sep 80	81 TFS/TFB 8	N K	AIM-9P	MiG-21MF/IrAF
24 Sep 80	81 TFS/TFB 8	?	AIM-54A	MiG-21MF/IrAF
25 Sep 80	TFB 8	?	AIM-54A	MiG-21/IrAF
25 Sep 80	TFB 8	?	AIM-9P	MiG-21/IrAF
25 Sep 80	TFB 8	?	AIM-9P	MiG-21/IrAF
25 Sep 80	72 TFS/TFB 7	S Naghdi	AIM-54A	MiG-23BN/IrAF
25 Sep 80	TFB 8	?	AAM	MiG-23BN/IrAF
2 Oct 80	TFB 8	?	AIM-9P	Su-20/IrAF
3 Oct 80	TFB 8	?	AAM	MiG-23/IrAF
5 Oct 80	TFB 8	?	?	Su-20/IrAF
5 Oct 80	TFB 8	?	?	Su-20/IrAF
5 Oct 80	TFB 8	?	?	MiG-23/IrAF
10 Oct 80	TFB 8	?	?	MiG-23BN/IrAF
10 Oct 80	TFB 8	?	?	MiG-23BN/IrAF
10 Oct 80	TFB 8	?	?	MiG-23BN/IrAF
12 Oct 80	**TFB 8**	**?**	**AIM-9P**	**Su-20/IrAF**
13 Oct 80	TFB 8	A Afshar	AAM	MiG-23BN/IrAF
15 Oct 80	TFB 8	?	AIM-7E-4	Su-20/IrAF
18 Oct 80	81 TFS/TFB 8	G Malej	AIM-9P	MiG-23/IrAF
18 Oct 80	81 TFS/TFB 8	G Malej	AIM-9P	MiG-23/IrAF
20 Oct 80	81 TFS/TFB 8	H All-e-Agha	AIM-7E-4	MiG-21MF/IrAF
22 Oct 80	81 TFS/TFB 8	K Sedghi	AIM-9P	MiG-23ML/IrAF
22 Oct 80	81 TFS/TFB 8	?	AIM-9	MiG-23BN/IrAF
25 Oct 80	81 TFS/TFB 8	?	AIM-9P	Su-20/IrAF
25 Oct 80	**81 TFS/TFB 8**	**?**	**AIM-7E-4**	**Su-20/IrAF (damaged)**
26 Oct 80	81 TFS/TFB 8	A Hazin	AIM-9P	MiG-21MF/IrAF
26 Oct 80	81 TFS/TFB 8	K Akhbari	AIM-9P	MiG-21MF/IrAF
29 Oct 80	81 TFS/TFB 8	K Sedghi	AIM-54A	MiG-23ML/IrAF
29 Oct 80	81 TFS/TFB 8	K Sedghi	AIM-54A	MiG-23ML/IrAF
29 Oct 80	81 TFS/TFB 8	K Sedghi	AIM-9P	MiG-23ML/IrAF
29 Oct 80	81 TFS/TFB 8	K Sedghi	AIM-9P	MiG-23ML/IrAF
10 Nov 80	81 TFS/TFB 8	?	AIM-7E-4	MiG-23/IrAF
21 Nov 80	TFB 8	A Afshar	AIM-7E-4	MiG-21/IrAF
27 Nov 80	TFB 8	A Afshar	AIM-54A	MiG-21/IrAF
? Nov 80	**TFB 8**	**?**	**AIM-54A***	**fighter, IrAF**
? Nov 80	**TFB 8**	**?**	**AIM-54A***	**fighter, IrAF**
2 Dec 80	82 TFS/TFB 8	F Dehghan	AIM-54A	MiG-21MF/IrAF
10 Dec 80	TFB 8	?	?	Su-20/IrAF
22 Dec 80	TFB 8	?	AIM-54A	MiG-21 or Su-20/IrAF

Date	Unit	Aircrew	Weapon	Victim/Country
22 Dec 80	TFB 8	?	AIM-54A	MiG-21 or Su-20/IrAF
30 Dec 80	TFB 8	?	?	MiG-21/IrAF
7 Jan 81	TFB 8	?	AIM-54A	MiG-23/IrAF
7 Jan 81	TFB 8	?	AIM-54A*	MiG-23/IrAF
7 Jan 81	TFB 8	?	AIM-54A*	MiG-23/IrAF
7 Jan 81	**TFB 8**	**?**	**AIM-54A***	**MiG-23/IrAF**
29 Jan 81	TFB 6	?	AIM-54	Su-20/IrAF
1 Apr 81	TFB 6	?	AIM-9P	MiG-23BN/IrAF
4 Apr 81	TFB 6	?	AIM-9P	MiG-23BN/IrAF
21 Apr 81	TFB 6	?	AIM-9P	MiG-23BN/IrAF
15 May 81	82 TFS/TFB 7	J Zandi	AIM-9P	MiG-21MF/IrAF
22 Oct 81	82 TFS/TFB 7	H Rostamil	AIM-54A	Mirage F 1EQ, 92 FS/IRAF
22 Oct 81	82 TFS/TFB 7	H Rostamil	AIM-54A	Mirage F 1EQ, 92 FS/IRAF
22 Oct 81	82 TFS/TFB 7	H Rostamil	AIM-54A	Mirage F 1EQ, 92 FS/IRAF
22 Oct 81	**82 TFS/TFB 7**	**Hadavand**	**AIM-54A**	**Mirage F 1EQ, 92 FS/IRAF**
22 Oct 81	82 TFS/TFB 7	H Rostamil	AIM-7E	MiG-21MF, 92 FS/IRAF
3 Dec 81	**TFB 8**	**withheld**	**?**	**Mirage F 1EQ, 92 FS/IRAF**
3 Dec 81	**TFB 8**	**withheld**	**?**	**Mirage F 1EQ, 92 FS/IRAF**
11 Dec 81	82 TFS/TFB 8	H All-e-Agha	AIM-54A	Mirage F 1EQ, 92 FS/IRAF
11 Dec 81	**82 TFS/TFB 8**	**H All-e-Agha**	**AIM-54A**	**Mirage F 1EQ, 92 FS/IRAF**
11 Dec 81	TFB 8	R Azad	AIM-54A	MiG-21MF/IrAF
11 Dec 81	**TFB 8**	**R Azad**	**AIM-54A**	**MiG-21MF/IrAF**
? Jan 82	82 TFS/TFB 8	J Zandi	AAM	MiG-21MF/IrAF
? Mar 82	72 TFS/TFB 1	?	AIM-9P	Su-22/IrAF
4 Apr 82	**TFB 8**	**?**	**AIM-9P**	**MiG-23/IrAF**
4 Apr 82	**TFB 8**	**?**	**AIM-9P**	**MiG-23/IrAF**
21 Jul 82	82 TFS/TFB 8	Toufanian	AIM-54A*	MiG-23MS/IrAF
21 Jul 82	82 TFS/TFB 8	Toufanian	AIM-54A*	MiG-23MS/IrAF
21 Jul 82	81 TFS/TFB 8	Moussavi	AIM-54A	Su-22/IrAF
16 Sep 82	TFB 8	S Rostami	AIM-54A	MiG-25RB, 1 FRS/IrAF
10 Oct 82	TFB 8	J Zandi	AIM-54A	MiG-23/IrAF
10 Oct 82	TFB 8	J Zandi	AIM-54A	MiG-23/IrAF
7 Nov 82	TFB 8	?	AIM-7E-4	Su-22M-3K/IrAF
21 Nov 82	TFB 8	M Khosrodad	AIM-54A	MiG-23MS/IrAF
21 Nov 82	TFB 8	M Khosrodad	AIM-54A	MiG-23MS/IrAF
21 Nov 82	TFB 8	M Khosrodad	AIM-7E-4	MiG-21/IrAF
27 Nov 82	TFB 8	?	AAM	SA 321/IrAF
1 Dec 82	TFB 8	S Rostami	AIM-54A	MiG-25RB, 17 FS/IrAF
4 Dec 82	81 TFS/TFB 8	Toufanian	AIM-54A	MiG-25PD, 1 FRS/IrAF
16 Jan 83	TFB 8	?	AIM-54A	MiG-23BN/IrAF
16 Jan 83	**TFB 8**	**?**	**AIM-54A**	**MiG-23BN/IrAF**
16 Jan 83	TFB 8	?	AIM-54A	fighter/IrAF
16 Jan 83	TFB 8	?	AIM-54A	fighter/IrAF
21 Jan 83	**?**	**?**	**AAM**	**fighter/IrAF**
21 Jan 83	**?**	**?**	**AAM**	**fighter/IrAF**
27 Jan 83	73 TFS/TFB 7	?	AAM	Su-20/IrAF
29 Jan 83	73 TFS/TFB 7	?	AAM	MiG-23MS/IrAF
14 Feb 83	**TFB 8**	**?**	**AAM**	**fighter/IrAF**
26 Feb 83	**72 TFS/TFB 1**	**?**	**AAM**	**Mirage F 1EQ/IrAF**
? Jun 83	82 TFS/TFB 8	Afkhami	AAM	MiG-23/IrAF
28 Jul 83	81 TFS/TFB 8	?	AAM	Mirage F 1EQ/IrAF
28 Jul 83	81 TFS/TFB 8	?	AAM	Mirage F 1EQ/IrAF
6 Aug 83	81 TFS/TFB 8	?	AIM-54A	MiG-25PD/IrAF (shared)
31 Aug 83	73 TFS/TFB 7	?	AAM	Su-22M-3K/IrAF
31 Aug 83	73 TFS/TFB 7	withheld	AAM	Su-22M-3K/IrAF
? Sep 83	**82 TFS/TFB 8**	**J Zandi**	**AAM**	**Su-22/IrAF**
? Sep 83	**82 TFS/TFB 8**	**J Zandi**	**AAM**	**Su-22/IrAF**
? Oct 83	**82 TFS/TFB 8**	**Afkhami**	**AAM**	**MiG-23/IrAF**
25 Feb 84	**TFB 8**	**C E**	**AIM-54A**	**MiG-21/IrAF**
25 Feb 84	**TFB 8**	**C E**	**AIM-54A**	**Su-20/22/IrAF**
25 Feb 84	**TFB 8**	**C E's wingman**	**AIM-54A**	**Su-20/22/IrAF**
25 Feb 84	**TFB 8**	**C E**	**AIM-54A**	**MiG-21/IrAF**

Date	Unit	Aircrew	Weapon	Victim/Air Force
1 Mar 84	**81 FS/TFB 8**	**withheld**	**AIM-54A**	**Su-22M/IrAF**
25 Mar 84	73 TFS/TFB 7	withheld	AIM-54A	Tu-22B, 8 BS/IrAF
6 Apr 84	81 TFS/TFB 8	?	AIM-54A	Tu-22B, 8 BS/IrAF
6 Apr 84	81 TFS/ TFB 8	?	AIM-54A	Tu-22B, 8 BS/IrAF
? Jun 84	82 TFS/TFB 8	Afkhami	AAM	Su-22/IrAF
26 Jul 84	**81 TFS/TFB 8**	**withheld**	**AIM-54A**	**Super Etendard/IrAF**
7 Aug 84	**81 TFS/TFB 8**	**withheld**	**AIM-54A**	**Super Etendard/IrAF**
11 Jan 85	**?**	**?**	**AAM**	**AM 39 Exocet/IrAF**
? Mar 85	**81 TFS/TFB 8**	**withheld**	**AIM-54A**	**MiG-27/VVS**
? Mar 85	81 TFS/TFB 8	withheld	AIM-54A	MiG-27/VVS
? Mar 85	81 TFS/TFB 8	withheld	AIM 54A	MiG-27/VVS
26 Mar 85	82 TFS/TFB 8	?	AAM	Mirage F 1EQ/IrAF
26 Mar 85	82 TFS/TFB 8	?	AAM	Mirage F 1EQ/IrAF
26 Mar 85	82 TFS/TFB 8	?	AAM	Mirage F 1EQ/IrAF
3 Jun 85	**72 TFS/TFB 1**	**?**	**AIM-54A**	**MiG-25RB/IrAF (damaged)**
20 Aug 85	**TFB 8**	**?**	**AIM-54A**	**MiG-23RB/IrAF**
14 Feb 86	**TFB 8**	**?**	**AAM**	**SA 321GV/IrAF**
15 Feb 86	TFB 8	?	AIM-54A	MiG-25RB/IrAF
16 Feb 86	TFB 8	?	AIM-54A	Tu-22B/IrAF
18 Feb 86	72 TFB/TFB 7	?	AIM-54A	Mirage F 1EQ/IrAF
14 Mar 86	82 TFS/TFB 8	Toufanian	AIM-9P	Mirage 5, 71 FS/EAF
? Apr 86	82 TFS/TFB 8	J Zandi	AAM	MiG-23/IrAF
? Apr 86	82 TFS/TFB 8	J Zandi	AIM-54A	MiG-23PD/IrAF
12 Jul 86	TFB 6	Reza	AIM-7E-4	MiG-23ML/IrAF
? Aug 86	TFB 8	?	AAM	Su-22/IrAF
? Aug 86	TFB 8	?	AAM	Su-22/IrAF
? Aug 86	TFB 8	?	AAM	Su-22/IrAF
? Aug 86	TFB 8	?	AAM	MiG-23/IrAF
? Aug 86	TFB 8	?	AAM	MiG-23/IrAF
6 Oct 86	TFB 6	?	AIM-54A	Mirage F 1EQ/IrAF
6 Oct 86	TFB 6	?	Manoeuvre	Mirage F 1EQ/IrAF
7 Oct 86	TFB 6	A Afshar	AAM	Mirage F 1EQ/IrAF
7 Oct 86	TFB 6	Afshar's wingman	AAM	Mirage F 1EQ/IrAF
14 Oct 86	81 TFS/TFB 8	?	AIM-54A	MiG-23/IrAF
? ? 86	73 TFS/TFB 7	?	AIM-54A	MiG-25BM/VVS
23 Jan 87	81 TFS/TFB 8	Moslemi	AIM-7E-4	MiG-23ML/IrAF
23 Jan 87	81 TFS/TFB 8	M Zooghi	AIM-9P	MiG-23ML/IrAF
23 Jan 87	**81 TFS/TFB 8**	**M Zooghi**	**AIM-7E-4**	**MiG-23ML/IrAF**
18 Feb 87	73 TFS/TFB 7	H Agha	AIM-7E-4	Mirage F 1EQ/IrAF
18 Feb 87	73 TFS/TFB 7	H Agha	AIM-9P	Mirage F 1EQ/IrAF
18 Feb 87	73 TFS/TFB 7	H Agha	AIM-54A	Mirage F 1EQ/IrAF
20 Feb 87	81 TFS/TFB 6	Amiraslani	AIM-54A	Mirage F 1EQ/IrAF
20 Feb 87	**TFB 6**	**?**	**AAM**	**Mirage F 1EQ/IrAF**
20 Feb 87	**TFB 6**	**?**	**AAM**	**Mirage F 1EQ/IrAF**
24 Feb 87	?	?	AAM	MiG-23ML/IrAF
24 Feb 87	?	?	AAM	Mirage F 1EQ-2/IrAF
? Feb 87	72 TFS/TFB 1	A Afshar	AIM-54	Su-22/IrAF
? Mar 87	**TFB 8**	**?**	**AIM-7E-4**	**AM 39 Exocet/IrAF**
? May 87	TFB 8	A Rahnavard	AIM-7E-4	Su-22/IrAF
24 Jun 87	**TFB 6**	**?**	**AIM-54A**	**SA 321H/IrAF**
22 Aug 87	82 TFS/TFB 8	Afkhami	AAM	MiG-23/IrAF
29 Aug 87	82 TFS/TFB 8	J Zandi	AAM	Mirage F 1EQ-5/IrAF
31 Aug 87	82 TFS/TFB 8	?	AAM	Mirage F 1EQ-5/IrAF
31 Aug 87	**82 TFS/TFB 8**	**?**	**AAM**	**Mirage F 1EQ-5/IrAF**
1 Sep 87	**TFB 8**	**?**	**AAM**	**fighter/IrAF**
1 Sep 87	**TFB 8**	**?**	**AAM**	**fighter/IrAF**
18 Sep 87	**TFB 8**	**?**	**AIM-54A**	**Mirage F 1EQ/IrAF**
16 Oct 87	**TFB 7**	**?**	**AAM**	**Mirage F 1EQ/IrAF**
17 Oct 87	TFB 8	withheld	AIM-9	MiG-23BK/IrAF
17 Oct 87	TFB 8	withheld	AIM-9	MiG-23BK/IrAF
17 Oct 87	TFB 8	withheld	AIM-9	MiG-23BK/IrAF
4 Nov 87	TFB 8	withheld	AIM-9	Su-22M-4K/IrAF

Date	Unit	Aircrew	Weapon	Victim/Country
11 Nov 87	72 TFS/TFB 1	?	AIM-54A	MiG-25BM/VVS
15 Nov 87	81 TFS/TFB 8	Afkhami	AIM-7	Mirage F1EQ-5/IrAF
15 Nov 87	**81 TFS/TFB8**	**Afkhami**	**AIM-7**	**Mirage F 1EQ-5/IrAF**
? Feb 88	82 TFS/ TFB 6	J Zandi	AIM-9P	Mirage F 1EQ/IrAF
? Feb 88	**82 TFS/TFB 6**	**J Zandi**	**AIM-9P**	**Mirage F 1EQ/IrAF**
9 Feb 88	82 TFS/TFB 6	Qiyassi	AIM-7E-4	Mirage F 1EQ-5/IrAF
9 Feb 88	82 TFS/TFB 6	Qiyassi	AIM-9P	Mirage F 1EQ-5/IrAF
9 Feb 88	82 TF/TFB 6	Qiyassi	AIM-9P	Mirage F 1EQ/IrAF
15 Feb 88	81 TFS/TFB 8	Toufanian	AIM-54A	Mirage F 1EQ/IrAF
16 Feb 88	TFB 8	A Rahnavard	AIM-9P	Mirage F 1EQ/IrAF
16 Feb 88	TFB 8	A Rahnavard	AIM-9P	Mirage F 1EQ/IrAF
25 Feb 88	TFB 8	G Esmaeli	AIM-54A	B-6D/IrAF
25 Feb 88	TFB 8	G Esmaeli	AIM-54A	C 601, AshM/IrAF
1 Mar 88	82 TFS/TFB 8	?	AAM	Su-20/IrAF
3 Mar 88	**TFB 8**	**?**	**AAM**	**Su-20/IrAF**
18 Mar 88	81 TFS/TFB 6	?	AAM	Mirage F 1EQ/IrAF
19 Mar 88	81 TFS/TFB 6	?	AIM-54A	MiG-23ML/IrAF
19 Mar 88	81 TFS/TFB 8	?	AIM-54A	Tu-22B, 7 BS/IrAF
19 Mar 88	81 TFS/TFB 8	?	AIM-54A	MiG-25RB, 1 FRS/IrAF
20 Mar 88	72 TFS/TFB 8	?	AIM-54A	MiG-25RB, 1 FRS/IrAF
22 Mar 88	72 TFS/TFB 8	?	AIM-54A	MiG-25RB, 1 FRS/IrAF
24 Mar 88	72 TFS/TFB 1	?	AAM	Mirage F 1EQ/IrAF
15 May 88	72 TFS/TFB 1	A Afshar	AIM-9P	Mirage F 1EQ/IrAF
9 Jul 88	81 TFS/TFB 8	M Zooghi	AIM-9P	Mirage F1EQ/IrAF

Note

* added to AIM-54 in column headed 'Weapon' designates multiple kills scored by the same missile. Three cases are known where a single AIM-54 destroyed two or more Iraqi fighters, including one in which three MiG-23BNs were shot down and the fourth damaged, and two in which two MiG-23s were shot down by a single AIM-54. However, we have added only two such cases to the list as we do not know anything more specific about the third case, except that it occurred sometime in October or November 1980

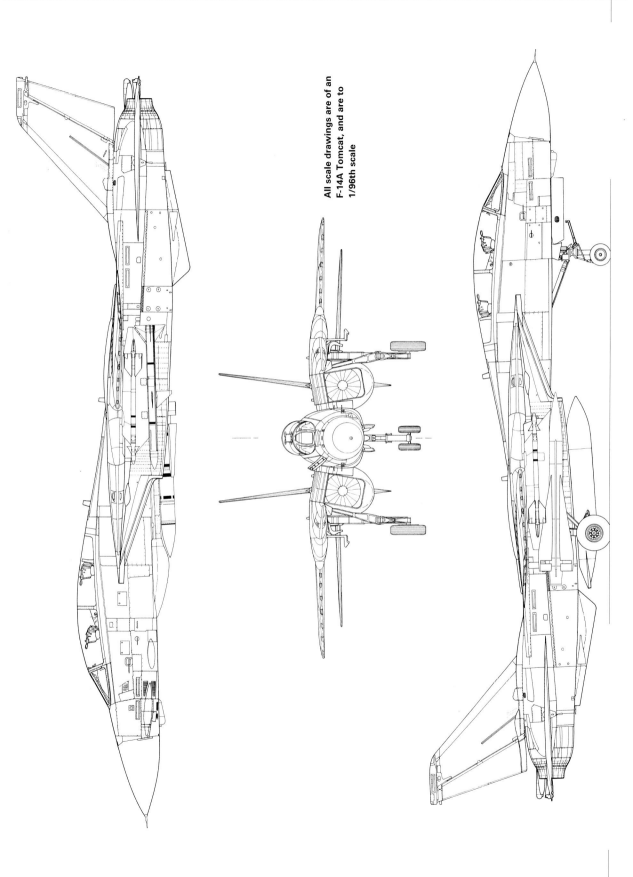

All scale drawings are of an
F-14A Tomcat, and are to
1/96th scale

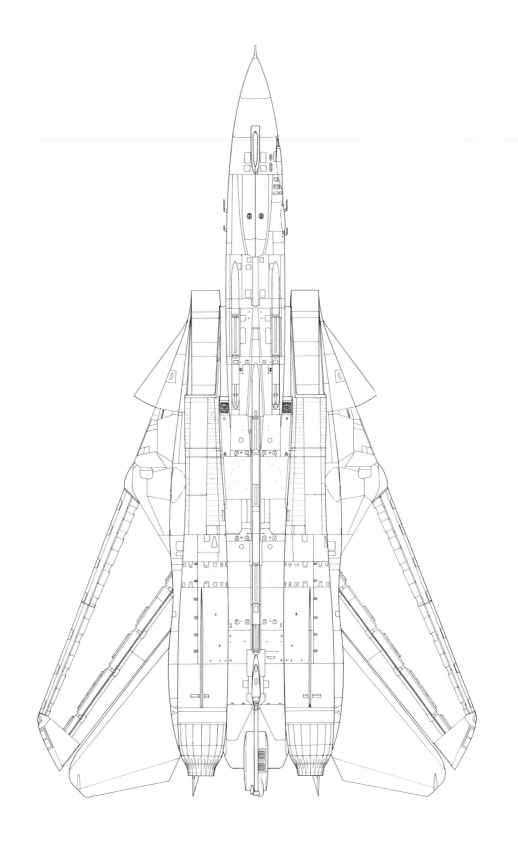

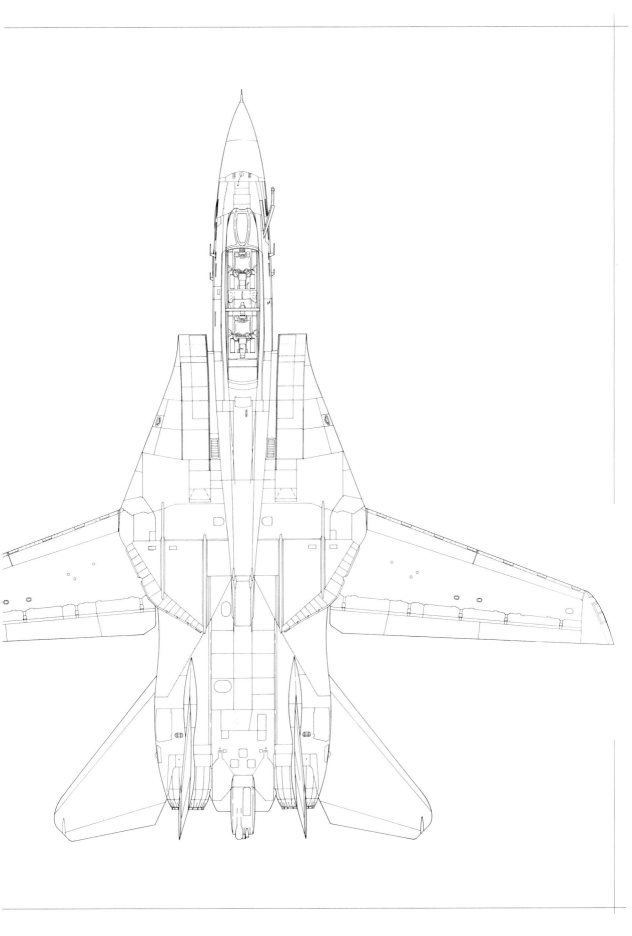

COLOUR PLATES

1
F-14A BuNo 160299/3-6001 (provisionally 3-863 in the USA), TFB 8, 1981
The first F-14A built for Iran, this aircraft was used for a relatively short time by the IIAF and then placed in storage at Khatami air base, where it remained for several years. In 1981 it was refurbished and returned to operational condition using parts supplied clandestinely by the US government. The aircraft was to participate in a number of aerial combats over the next few years, downing at least two Iraqi fighters while in service with the 81st and 82nd TFSs. Its final fate remains unknown.

2
F-14A BuNo 160318/3-6020, TFB 8, 1986
The 20th Tomcat supplied to Iran, 3-6020 became one of the most successful of the conflict with Iraq. Surviving the chaotic revolutionary period in operational condition, it saw extensive wartime service from September 1980 onwards. Remaining in the frontline until war's end in July 1988, the fighter is known to have shot down at least ten Iraqi aircraft. 3-6020 was the first F-14A to have fired an AIM-54A at an Iraqi MiG-25, on 15 May 1981. The Phoenix missed, but only after the IrAF pilot had accelerated to 2800 kmh (1750 mph) in an effort to outrun the missile. Apart from its combat service, this Tomcat was also used in the Iranian 'Bombcat' trials when, in 1986, tests were conducted with Mk 83 bombs carried on under-fuselage mountings in place of AIM-54s. Despite rumours suggesting that F-14s dropped bombs in anger, the authors have yet to find any corroborating evidence to prove that Iranian Tomcats were indeed used on air-to-ground missions during the war. It is known that at least two jets undertook the bomb trials, and that in July 1988 the US Navy issued a corresponding warning to the commanders of its warships operating in the Persian Gulf. 3-6020 survived the war, and was completely overhauled by IACI several years ago. It emerged from rework in the now standard blue-grey camouflage scheme applied to all IRIAF F-14As.

3
F-14A BuNo 160320/3-6022, 82nd TFS, TFB 8, 1981
This particular Tomcat shot down two Iraqi MiG-23MSs with a single AIM-54A missile on 21 July 1982 in an engagement fought halfway between Baghdad and the Iranian border after its crew ignored orders not to enter Iraqi airspace. The jet was subsequently used to destroy at least five other Iraqi fighters during the course of the war. 3-6022 was completely overhauled post-war, and duly became one of the first Tomcats to be repainted in the new camouflage colours in 1995. It presently remains in frontline service with the IRIAF.

4
F-14A BuNo 160322/3-6024, 81st TFS, TFB 8, 1978
In October 1978, while in IIAF service, this aircraft was one of two Tomcats which intercepted a Soviet MiG-25RBS high over the Caspian Sea and tracked it for two minutes as the Soviet pilot did his best to accelerate away from the intercepting Grumman fighters. 3-6024 went on to see extensive service with the 81st TFS during the war with Iraq, and was credited with the destruction of several Iraqi fighters, including at least one Mirage F 1EQ. It currently remains in service with TFB 8, having recently been overhauled and repainted in blue-grey camouflage.

5
F-14A BuNo 160325/3-6027, TFB 7, 1977
Displaying IIAF titling on its right side, 3-6027 was one of the first Tomcats issued to the Imperial Iranian Air Force at TFB 7 in 1976. It was used extensively during the training of early Iranian Tomcat crews.

6
F-14A BuNo 160325/3-6027, 72nd TFS, TFB 7, 1980
Marked with IRIAF titling in early 1980, 3-6027 is known to have been used by a detachment from the 72nd TFS (a unit equipped with F-4Ds from late 1980) in the first weeks of the war with Iraq. The jet was usually deployed to Mehrabad air base, where a handful of Tomcats were stationed for training, testing and, on occasion, the defence of Tehran. At least three F-14s (possibly including 3-6027) were also used as 'mini-AWACS' and airborne fighter-directors, controlling F-4s from TFB 1 as they intercepted Iraqi MiG-25s, Tu-16s and Tu-22s. The final fate of 3-6027 remains unknown.

7
F-14A BuNo 160330/3-6032, 81st TFS, TFB 8, 1986
This Tomcat was one of several known to have changed squadrons during the course of the war with Iraq. Initially assigned to TFB 7, it was amongst the first F-14s to be totally overhauled in Iran and, from 1986, was assigned to the 81st TFS. Used in January 1987 to down an Iraqi MiG-23, the aircraft is depicted here in artwork boasting a war load of two AIM-54As and four AIM-9Ps – a normal configuration for Tomcats hunting MiG-25s, B-6s (Tu-16s) or Tu-22s. In such cases, IRIAF crews tried to keep their aircraft's weight as low as possible in an effort to save fuel for high-speed pursuits. This configuration was used successfully on a number of occasions, resulting in the destruction of at least four MiG-25s. The final fate of 3-6032 remains unknown.

8
F-14A BuNo 160337/3-6039, 82nd TFS, TFB 8, 1987
This aircraft was used by Capt Amiraslani to shoot down the IrAF Mirage F 1EQ flown by 1Lt Ahlan at

long range with a single AIM-54A on 20 February 1987. The son of Brig Gen Hekmat Abdel Qadr, Ahlan was killed. Amiraslani had been thrown out of the IRIAF after the revolution, but he was later permitted to return, and became only the second or third Iranian pilot to fire a live AIM-54A in training in his own country. The fate of 3-6039 remains unknown.

9
F-14A BuNo 160345/3-6047, TFB 7, 1980
This Tomcat was seen in several photographs, and observed by foreigners in Iran, both before and after the revolution. In 1986 it was seen taking off from Tabriz (TFB 2), in northern Iran, on a CAP carrying a single AIM-54A, two Sparrows and two Sidewinders. Little is known about its service during the war, except that it was originally assigned to TFB 7.

10
F-14A BuNo 160350/3-6052, TFB 7, 1986
Originally assigned to the 73rd TFS, this jet spent most of the war at Hor air base (TFB 7), near Shiraz. Few details have emerged pertaining to its wartime service, other than that it was used in February 1986 to shoot down at least one Iraqi MiG-25. 3-6052's final fate also remains unknown.

11
F-14A BuNo 160361/3-6063, TFB 7 and 8, 1987
Initially delivered to the 73rd TFS and based at Hor, 3-6063 spent several years in storage before being returned to service some time in the mid 1980s. It was then sent to the Mehrabad-based 72nd TFS detachment, where the jet was last seen in 1987.

12
F-14A BuNo 160371/3-6073, TFB 1, 1987
Originally issued to the 82nd TFS, this Tomcat was one of three used for Project *Sky Hawk*, which was intended to make the MIM-23B I-HAWK/Sedjil SAM compatible with the F-14, and its AWG-9 radar. In addition, 3-6073 was also used to test the Yasser guided air-to-ground missile (seen here mounted on the left underwing pylon), which essentially comprises the MIM-23's body mated with the warhead of the M-117 general purpose bomb. Yasser was successfully tested, and it is currently operational with the IRIAF. This aircraft is notable for being one of only a small number of Tomcats to display the IRIAF symbol on its fin above the national flag. The aircraft remains in service, and is still used for various testing purposes.

13 & 14 (nose scrap view)
F-14A BuNo 160377/3-6079, 81st and 82nd TFS, TFB 8, 1980 and 1982 (scrap view)
Probably the most successful Tomcat ever built, 3-6079 was the last F-14 delivered to Iran – 3-6080 was held back in the USA for testing after the Iranian revolution and was never delivered. Following its delivery 3-6079 was put in storage,

but it returned to service with the 81st TFS in September 1980, at which point it was still wearing IIAF titles, although without the national flag on the fin. The jet was used to shoot down an Iraqi MiG-21 and a MiG-23 just weeks later. By year-end it was seen wearing IRIAF titles, but again without the national flag on the fin – this appears to have been applied in late 1981 or early 1982. Its markings were 'complete' by 9 February 1988, when 1Lt Qiyassi used it to shoot down three Iraqi Mirage F 1EQs during two engagements in two hours. 3-6079 remains in service with the 82nd TFS.

15
F-14A BuNo 160320/3-6022, TFB 8, 1996
This aircraft was the first F-14A to display the IRIAF's new blue-grey camouflage scheme. It was overhauled and repainted with polyurethane-based paint by IACI in 1995, before being displayed at Mehrabad air base the following February. At that time, the IRIAF was still experimenting with this camouflage pattern, and 3-6022 is also known to have received tan and light blue-grey colours similar to those applied to Iranian MiG-29s in the early 1990s. The jet's low visibility serials are barely discernible even from a distance of just a few metres.

Back cover
F-14A BuNo 160322/3-6024, TFB 8, 2002
Depicted here in the scheme applied shortly after a lengthy overhaul at IACI, this aircraft wears similar camouflage to 3-6022, except that its serial has been applied in flat black – all surviving, and refurbished, Iranian Tomcats, including 3-6020 and 3-6041, have also been marked with flat black serials. All repainted aircraft also retain their original BuNos, albeit applied in low-visibility numerals, in the original location beneath the stabilators as specified by the US Navy.

COLOUR SECTION

1
With wings fully spread, and showing the 'Asia Minor' camouflage pattern to advantage, F-14A BuNo 160299 is seen at low speed during flight testing. Note that the leading edges of the wings, horizontal stabilators and vertical stabilisers have been left unpainted. Also of interest is the chin-mounted IRST set, which was never actually purchased by the IIAF despite serious offers from the USA (*Grumman via authors*)

2
BuNo 160378 was the 80th, and last, F-14A built for Iran. The aircraft was held in the USA and scheduled for conversion to the USAF style 'boom-and-receptacle' in-flight refuelling system. In the

end it was neither converted nor delivered. When the Shah was overthrown, the aircraft was put into storage at the AMARC facility at Davis-Monthan air base in Arizona. In 1986 it was refurbished and brought up to US Navy standard at NADEP North Island, after which it was issued to the PMTC on 13 November 1987. Later, the jet was used by the NAWC and the Weapons Test Squadron at Point Mugu (*authors' collection*)

3

Tomcat 3-6051 (furthest from the camera) and two other F-14As are seen on the tarmac at Khatami soon after their delivery from Grumman. The revolution not only thwarted plans to purchase additional Tomcats, but almost resulted in the Iranian Tomcat fleet being sold back to the US in 1979 (*authors' collection*)

4

In the months prior to the 1979 revolution which swept the Shah of Iran from power, three F-14 units were declared fully operational. The additional training of crews, particularly in in-flight refuelling operations, was also in full swing by then. KC 707-3J9C 5-8301, also known as *Shabaviz 1*, is seen here tanking two F-14As from TFB 7 high over the central Iranian desert (*Grumman*)

5

Capt Barekat was one of Iran's first F-14 pilots. Highly trained and motivated, IIAF air and groundcrew had little difficulty in qualifying on the complex Tomcat (*IIAF Association via authors*)

6

For the duration of the Iran-Iraq War, Western press reports declared that Iranian F-14s had been 'sabotaged, and were thus unable to operate AIM-54s', were 'not very effective' and were 'lacking even routine items such as brakes and tyres'. Meanwhile, in the USA discussion raged about the feasibility of the F-14 and the AIM-54, yet the IRIAF put its Tomcats, and all their capabilities, to good use – so much so that they are known to have scored 37 air-to-air kills within the first three months of the war, including at least ten with Phoenix missiles. Aircraft 3-6079 – the last F-14 supplied to Iran – is seen here during the early stages of the war wearing IRIAF titles and the TFB 8 symbol on the fin, but without the Iranian flag. It also carries a full war-load of four Phoenix, two Sidewinders and two Sparrows (*authors' collection*)

7

Iranian F-14As were described as 'non-operational', 'canabilised for spares', 'lacking AWG-9' and 'unable to operate AIM-54s' by the Western specialist aviation press for much of the 1980s, yet 3-6051 is seen here equipped with two AIM-54As and four AIM-9Ps on patrol along the northern Iranian border during the height of the war with Iraq. Although capable of intercepting enemy aircraft at considerable distances, Phoenix missiles were not always used to open aerial engagements. Indeed, on 18 February 1987, Capt H Agha shot down three Mirage F 1EQs over the Persian Gulf. The first fell to Sparrows and the second to a Sidewinder. Only then did the Iranian pilot fire his two AIM-54s at the last two Iraqis while they were already fleeing. One scored a direct hit and the other passed only a few metres ahead of the target but failed to detonate (*authors' collection*)

8

TFB 8 crews pose with 3-6053 in 1985–86. Despite severe maltreatment by the regime, most Iranian Tomcat pilots remained determined to do their duty for their country by fighting the Iraqis at every possible opportunity. Although somewhat hamstrung by the unreliability of its TF30 engines, the F-14A remains a great favourite with all those who flew it – and those that still do (*authors' collection*)

9

Four combat-weary TFB 8 pilots pose in front of 3-6060. CAPs lasting up to 12 hours in duration, political pressure from the ruling regime and repeated encounters with a numerically-stronger enemy have made these men look at least ten years older than they are. Despite these operational stresses, IRIAF pilots were still able to develop their skills, including the ability to dogfight the F-14 at high AOA settings and very low speeds. Such manoeuvres may have been considered too dangerous by the US Navy, but IRIAF pilots used them on a daily basis. By employing such tactics, Tomcat crews could not only survive engagements with up to 14 Iraqi fighters, but also regularly score kills (*authors' collection*)

10

Tomcat 3-6060 is seen on display in Tehran post-war. This aircraft was one of the F-14As which frustrated seven consecutive Iraqi attempts to attack Iranian shipping convoys in the northern Persian Gulf on 9 February 1988. Prior to that, it had also participated in Project *Sky Hawk*, as well as the 'Bombcat' trials (*authors' collection*)

11

Two ATM-7 Sparrow training rounds are seen on display during the 'Holy War of Defence' exhibition held in Tehran in November 2001. IRIAF F-14s were seldom seen carrying Sparrows after the Iran-Iraq War. The weapon is a semi-active radar homing missile, which means that it homes on the reflection of a continuous wave radar signal transmitted by the fighter's radar antenna. This is separate to the basic signal emitted by the radar in search and track mode, and functions much like the guidance system of existing SAMs. Although scoring a number of kills using Sparrows, Iranian pilots were never convinced about their performance, experiencing numerous mechanical failures in combat. Additionally, illuminating the target until the missile had hit denied crews much needed flexibility in air combat. Nevertheless, locally modified variants of the AIM-7E-4 remain effective weapons with the IRIAF to this day (*authors' collection*)

12
Together with the Phoenix, the AIM-9P Sidewinder proved the deadliest weapon in the Iranian Tomcat's arsenal, enabling the aircraft to score at least 50 aerial victories. The Sidewinder became the most popular missile not only with the Iranians but also the Iraqis, who tried to obtain supplies from other Arab air forces. In Iranian service, the AIM-9P proved a reliable and deadly weapon, and IRIAF F-14 pilots sometimes flew their aircraft into combat armed only with two Sidewinders and the 20 mm gun. One pilot explained to the authors, 'The Tomcat was so superior to anything the Iraqis flew, and the Sidewinders and the gun were so effective, that we could confidently engage the enemy even if the AWG-9 radar was not functioning' (*authors' collection*)

13
Seldom seen in US Navy service, the ATM-54A training round shown here is still used by the IRIAF today. Although its effectiveness is still debated in the West, the Phoenix remains the most important aerial weapon in the IRIAF arsenal. Iran has even started limited production of a reverse-engineered version of this weapon fitted with upgraded avionics. According to US intelligence sources, it is considered 'comparable at least with the AIM-54C'. As a result, Iranian F-14As remain the most potent interceptors in the Middle East (*authors' collection*)

14
F-14A BuNo 160322/3-6024 is just one of many Iranian Tomcats to boast a rich service history. It not only shot down at least six Iraqi fighters, but also participated in the pursuit of a Soviet MiG-25R in the late summer of 1978 which led to the termination of the 'Foxbat' overflights of Iran (*authors' collection*)

15
A port view of 3-6024, displaying the new blue-grey camouflage scheme, at the 'Holy War of Defence' exhibition held in Tehran in November 2001. Note that the light blue colour now covers surfaces previously painted in sand, resulting in a pattern that is effectively a 'negative' of the old scheme (*authors' collection*)

16 & 17
These close-up views of the right rear side of 3-6024 reveal details of the markings and camouflage adopted by the IRIAF for its surviving Tomcats from the mid 1990s onward (*authors' collection*)

18
This close-up of the right side of the cockpit area shows the extended in-flight refuelling probe (without the doors) and all the stencilling in English, in standard US Navy positions (*authors' collection*)

INDEX

References to illustrations are shown in **bold**. Colour Section illustrations are prefixed 'cs.', with page and caption locators in brackets.